Republic Lost

Zionists Destroy the Union

Billy Ray Wilson

authorHOUSE®

AuthorHouse™
1663 Liberty Drive
Bloomington, IN 47403
www.authorhouse.com
Phone: 1-800-839-8640

First published by AuthorHouse 9/12/2011

ISBN: 978-1-4634-4855-4 (sc)
ISBN: 978-1-4634-4854-7 (e)

Library of Congress Control Number: 2011916043

Printed in the United States of America

TABLE OF CONTENTS

FOREWORD

This book will be my last attempt to enlighten the American people regarding Zionist control of the United States Government. To this end, unless the people rise up, the results will be the demise of a government by the people, for the people, of the people. Republic Lost.

With regards to Zionist control, Mr. Uri Avnery, a long time Israeli peace activist wrote in his news release "Deny! Deny!," dated June 19, 2011, the following:

"The one thing that all these brands ("Jewish State", "the nation-state of the Jewish people", or "State of the Jewish people.") have in common is that they are perfectly imprecise. What does "Jewish" mean? A nationality, a religion, a tribe? "Who are the Jewish people"? Or, even more vague, the "Jewish Nation?" Does this include the Congressmen who enact the laws of the United States? Or the cohorts of Jews who are in charge of US Middle East policy? Which country does the Jewish ambassador of the UK in Tel Aviv represent?"

My two previous books, MY STRUGGLE TOO and ENOUGH IS ENOUGH, were autobiographies, comments and questions: For example, I recommended a National Referendum be placed on a ballot during a presidential election year. The ballot would ask the American people the question: Can individuals residing and reaping the benefits of this great nation identify themselves by a religion versus American Citizenship?

My response to the question would be NO. The United States of

America is a physical entity established, regrettably in too many cases, forcefully against the indigenous population and, equally appalling, a blind eye toward indentured slaves and the sale of a human beings into slavery.

Religion on the other hand, regardless of the name of the religion, was/is a fabrication of a mythical entity handed down from one generation after another. In my books, I addressed Judaism, as individuals of this religion believe they are their Entity's (God of Abraham) Chosen People.

There may have been twenty books sold in book stores across the United States and the international community. One major book store chain would not physically display publications in their stores. A client had to know of the books, then he or she could order the book for home delivery.

Moreover, in my hometown library, the book is not on the shelves for checkout; however, if the party asks for the books, then he or she may check out the publication.

The books did not have vulgar stories or any material that could be construed as opposing the dictates of the United States Constitution or dispute/disclaim the Declaration of Independence's words that we are all equal in the United States. Without a doubt, in my opinion, lack of sales were because of the books were perceived to be anti-Semitic.

Anti-Semitic, I am not. I am an atheist. (In 2001, I was a Deist but the more I learned, I didn't fit as a Deist.) Americans can belief in and worship whatever religious entity he or she may choose; however, do not attempt to force your religion on me or inject religion into the administration of this great nation

One of the reasons I wrote the books was, hopefully, said writings would cease the flashbacks, anger and hate for our country's illegal war in the Kingdom of Laos and the hardships and torture our prisoners of war suffered.

In 1993, I sought medication and a mental health provider. I held in my feelings from 1973 to 1993. Today, I no longer cry for no reason and have very few periods of vulgar outbursts. However, my belief that once I retired from government employment, my stress would ease. In this light, work stress did ease but, with all the free time, I was able to become more involved in the political affairs of our country. My stress and frustration worsened.

With the free time, I began reading communications regarding the reasons the United States was at a constant state of aggression since the end of the Eisenhower Administration, especially in the Middle East. My findings led to former President Harry S. Truman, whom I consider a TRAITOR.

Hopefully, Americans will read this book and rise up and replace our government with a new government. When I write of rise up I mean go to the polls and vote for Americans . Americans, I might add, are those individuals, male or female, that understand the dictates of the United States Constitution and the spirit of the Declaration of Independence are the governing documents of our republic.

Our country is a Constitutional Republic which means, our large piece of North America belongs to the people.

BACKGROUND

In my opinion, the reader needs to know background, both personal and professional, to understand my knowledge and opinions of events, international history, religious background and my love for the United States of America.

I was born on September 21, 1943 at the home of an Aunt Eva Moore, East Bernstadt, Kentucky. She was a half sister of my father Raleigh Lee Wilson. My father was in the United States Marine Corps.

My mother was Abbie Brown, one of 14 children. There were 7 boys and 7 girls in mother's family.

I have two sisters, Janice Ruth and Pamela June.

Being a typical southeastern Kentuckian, my youth was one in which religious indoctrination was a daily affair. (Brainwashed if you will.) Respect and devotion to the United States of America based on the dictates of the United States Constitution and Declaration of Independence were instilled. Love for family was without question.

My father was a strong Republican almost to the point that the elephant could run and he would vote for the elephant. His brother was the same. I remember watching the election results between Adlai Stevenson, Democratic Governor of Illinois, and General of the Army Dwight David Eisenhower on television at an uncle's home in Ohio. A great night for our nation.

Regarding education, my mother allowed me to purchase books, assemble models, go to 4-H Camp and visit other aunts in Michigan and Ohio. I was free to learn, expect any subject dealing with sex.

After a number of years of physical separation, my mother and father divorced. She married an older gentlemen which naturally, he and I did not see eye to eye. To keep stress at a minimum at home, I joined the United States Air Force 9 days after I turned 17. My mother had to sign for me.

From September 20, 1960 through October 1, 1980, I served in the United States Air Force. My career was on continuous education. One could say the Strategic Air Command's Officers and enlisted supervisor were my father.

At Homestead Air Force Base, Homestead, Florida, I was fortunate or unfortunate, depending on one's opinion, to have been assigned to the Strategic Air Command's (SAC) 19th Combat Defense Squadron. Our squadron's task was to provide Law Enforcement for the non-flight line air base and assure the security of the strategic aircraft parked on the airbase's aprons.

Shortly following the Squadron's Army Combat Training, a new training initiative imposed by SAC; U.S. and Cuban refugees, trained by a U.S. Government Agency, attempted to over-throw the government of Fidel Castro. This incident was know as the Bay of Pigs.

The over-throw of Castro failed. The reasons were not that of planned operational assault, the forces dispatched against Castro or the U.S. military resources positioned at Homestead and other locations in the southern United States. The failure lies at the feet of President John F. Kennedy and his brother, Robert.

Regarding the buildup of U.S. Forces at Homestead, the 31st Tactical Fighter Wing moved from California to the air base. Instead of maintaining two separate command (Strategic Air Command and Tactical Air Command (TAC) airfield security teams, a decision was made to integrate TAC personnel into SAC's Security Forces to assure airfield security.

Of note, during the massive building up, I apprehended a non Air Force service member inside the family housing area. This individual prompted additional duty hours by the Law Enforcement team due to his acts inside base housing.

While on-patrol between Crash Gate 1 and Crash Gate 2, I apprehended a Spanish speaking individual walking toward the parked B-52 aircraft.

And, I don't remember the exact date but President Kennedy came to the airbase to award the Presidential Unit award to the 31st Tactical Fighter Wing. (Because TAC forces were integrated for our squadron's duties, the 19th Combat Defense Squadron received orders for the award.)

The day of the Kennedy's arrival, naturally security was beefed. Our squadron assigned security personnel to man the roadways traveled by the President's motorcade. I looked at the President at few feet when passing in the Presidential Limo. He looked really tired.

During the peace talks between the United States and Cuba, a U.S. Air Force Reserve Lieutenant Colonel would arrive at Homestead through the West Gate en-route to the aircraft that would fly him to Cuba. I was always posted at the gate for his arrival.

When an agreement was reached between the U.S. and Cuba, the prisoners of the Bay of Pigs assault arrived the airbase via U.S. aircraft. From the aircraft they were taken to the giant, black hangar where an administrative processing took place and money given to the returnees. From the base, the went by charted buses to Miami Beach for a coming home party.

Months after their return, a number of the former prisoners would visit the base, this time, as members of the U.S. Army.

On a personal note, I had a shotgun wedding at the Air Base Chapel. From the marriage came a daughter. Naturally, the marriage did not last.

And, regretfully, on the evening of December 31, 1959, I was driving down a wood lined, unmarked street that ending in a T-Intersection without street signs. Across the roadway were railroad tracks and a loading platform for the farmers to load their produce on the train. I failed to make a turn resulting in a damaged spine, lacerations, and comma.

What the assignment at Homestead revealed too me, the Executive and Legislative Branches of the U.S. Government, through their legal and illegal actions, force the U.S. military to resolve their political mistakes by the use and/or possible use of force. However, in the case of Cuba and President Raul

Castro's government, Zionist keep Cuba listed as a danger to the United States. Cuba is not now or ever been a threat to the United States.

From Homestead Air Force Base, myself and three airman from the Defense Squadron received transfer orders to Kunsan Air Base, Republic of South Korea (1964 - 1965).

Kunsan was a small, joint use air base with the South Korean Air Force. The nation was still on an alert from the war of aggression in Armistice status. United Nations and Communist powers still haven't signed a legal end to the Korean War. The reason we were there, in my opinion, was due to an alliance with the United Nations. Former President Thomas Jefferson warned not to enter into alliances. Truman was at the helm of state at the beginning of the war.

There are those Americans that feel if President Truman had not fired General of the Army Douglas Macarthur, the war on the Korean peninsula may have had a different outcome.

My next assignment in to a U.S. State Department induced military adventure was at Don Muang Royal Thai Air Base, Kingdom of Thailand (1966 - 1967).

Don Muang was a Thai Air Base located on the Bangkok International Airport reservation. At arrival there was no U.S. Air Force military housing or independent base administrative facilities. Structures on the Thai Air Base had been converted into administrative and support facilities.

The air traffic at Don Muang and the International Airport were heavy. The airport reservation was the shipping point for U.S. Logistics to South Vietnam, In-Country Thailand, and the Kingdom of Laos. Equally important, Don Muang was the home of US/Thai Air Defense Aircraft, Joint U.S./Thai Military Advisory Aircraft, KC-135 tankers and U.S. Navy special mission aircraft, not VIP support aircraft.

Again, in my opinion, Don Muang was part of a multi-year U.S. State Department Policy developed to support the Southeast Asia Treaty Organization (SEATO).

From Thailand, I returned to Kelly Air Force Base, San Antonio, TX (1966-1968). At Kelly we witnessed, first hand, the Department of Defense's interaction with the Military Industrial Complex. For example, our flight scheduling section provided aircrew support for ferry pilots delivering U.S. purchased/gratis aircraft to Central American countries. Also, we provided air transport to Flag Officers to watch the rolling out of a new C-5A by the aircraft's manufacturer.

On the sad side at Kelly, a house mate killed himself. The Sergeant had been assigned in Thailand where he had an affair with a Thai woman. His wife, in the United States, had an affair and became pregnant, The Sergeant wanted to forgive and forget but, allegedly, the Sergeant's mother was against the re-union. I found the Sergeant dead one afternoon at the end of the duty day. The Sergeant worked shift work.

Wanting to return to Southeast Asia, I volunteered for duty in South Vietnam and for any Special Assignment. I was notified I was selected for a Secret Assignment at a Southeast Asia location. The assignment would be in civilian clothing and require a Top Secret Clearance. Headquarters was at Bolling Air Force Base, Washington, DC. The assignment was known as Project 404.

The assignment, in my opinion, was once again in support of the United State Departments adventures outside the oversight of the Congress of the United States.

I fathered a son out-of-wedlock but did not leave him In-Country. I obtained custody of him and brought him to the United States. His mother did not want to leave her adopted home even after I told her the United States was going to leave Southeast Asia.

My In-Country Commander was able to arrange an assignment to Wurtsmith Air Force Base, Michigan (1973-1973) so I could be near my son. I had made arrangements with one of mother's sister to care for my son. He attended the Holy Redeemer Catholic Church/School Detroit.

SAC's leadership at Wurtsmith was typical of support provided to members of the Strategic Air Command whatever their reason. To this end, my son came with me as a Immigrant; whereas, I had to go to Federal Court in Alpena, Michigan to make my son an American citizen. I am deeply indebted to Wurtsmith's Base Commander and Air Operations Commander.

As you may have noted, the assignment at Wurtsmith was short. The reason is I learned of the formation of a Joint Service Command known as the Joint Casualty Resolution Center (JCRC), to be located at Nakhon Phanom Royal Thai Air Base, Kingdom of Thailand (1973 - 1974). The organization's mission was to recover the physical remains of U.S. Missing in Action

(MIA) from the Vietnam Era War and/or resolve status through the assets of the combined U.S. Government's Intelligence Agencies. To this end, as a former Command & Control Supervisor in the theatre, I had first hand knowledge of shoot downs and hostile activities at Southeast Asia's US/Indigenous sites, so I volunteered for the assignment.

A short time at the assignment, I learned from first hand experiences, that JCRC was a political assignment created by the Department of Defense to appease family members of the MIAs. However, I was able to locate classified information that allowed the status of MIA to be changed to KIA for a number of the missing.

Following the death of an Army Captain and the wounding of other military personnel, coupled with previous findings against the organization, I wrote the Commander asking to be reassigned or discharged as I would not waiver my beliefs taught me by the Strategic Air Command. I was reassigned to Pease Air Force Base, New Hampshire.

JCRC was an example of the deaths and injuries to American military personnel to appease members of Congress or the presidential administration in power.

Pease Air Force Base, New Hampshire (1974-1976) was a SAC Base. I knew what to expect regarding duties and integrity of the command. In this light, I wrote the later Senator John Tower regarding the JCRC assignment. Some months later, I received an invitation to meet with a Pentagon Investigation Board in Washington, DC. Command provided me with travel orders and per diem to attend the Pentagon Investigation. Some months following the Washington trip, I received orders for an Army Outstanding Unit Award.

While at Pease, I was sent on temporary duties to Andersen Air Base, Guam to support the Vietnamese Baby Airlift. The increase in air traffic was more than the assigned staff could handle.

And, while at Andersen, the Cambodian military had hijacked a ship and held the ship's crew hostage. The actions by the U.S. State Department once again were responsible for Americans and indigenous being killed and wounded.

My visit to the Pentagon further hardened my feelings for Flag Officers that appease legislative and executive branch official instead of saying no to illegal wars and un-Constitutional activities.

While in Guam, I met a number of Filipinos who were married to U.S. Service members so when I received orders for assignment to Clark Air Base, Republic of the Philippines, I had an ideal of what to expect. Also, once when transit through the Philippines en-route to Thailand I spent an overnight in Angeles City outside the air base.

Clark Air Base at the date of my assignment was the largest U.S. Air Force installation outside the Continental United States. There was a Flag Officer (General) billet as 13teen Air Force Commander. The Air Force Hospital was a regional hospital serving the greater portion of U.S. Southeast Asia military personnel. The air base maintained one of the best, if not the best, gunnery ranges in the world. The Air-To-Ground range was north of the air base. The Air-To-Air & Air-To-Water ranges were located a Poro Point, Philippines.

Air Wings from throughout the Pacific would send their best aircrews to Clark annually for the title of the Pacific's Best Aircrew. Nellis Air Force Base' Range, Las Vegas, NV, served the same purpose as Clark for the Continental United States.

Clark's Law Enforcement and Security Section had mounted horse and motorcycle patrols. Their services were needed due to the number of thefts, burglaries, etc., against Americans. Crimes against Americans was as great in the City of Angeles outside the airbase.

I was married while at Clark and our marriage lasted nearly 10 years.

Clark Air Base and the U.S. Naval Installations were closed following a massive volcano eruptions near Clark. Also, in truth, Clark and the naval bases were no longer needed due to our country's advancements in sea and air resources.

My last assignment was at Travis Air Force Base, Fairfield, CA (1978-1980). My command of assignment was the Air Force Logistic Command(AFLC). To this end, shortly after assignment, I submitted my request for retirement nearly years prior to date of retirement. (My head was and is messed up. I can no longer accept lies.)

Since my retirement, Air Force Commands such as SAC, TAC, AFLC names were changed to reflect, I suppose, the modern air force; however, in my opinion, when the names changed so did the integrity and honor of these once honorable commands.

While awaiting retirement orders, I learned the Northrup Aircraft Services Division, Hawthorne, CA were hiring Air Operations personnel to train Royal Saudi Air Force Warrant Officers. I applied and was hired by Northup followed with employment assignments with McDonnell Douglas Services. I was at King Khalid Air Base, Asir Province, Khamis Mushayt, Kingdom of Saudi Arabia for 6 non-consecutive years.

Of note, after a number of months at Khamis Mushayt, I began bleeding internally. I was hospitalized at Northrup's Medical Clinic, King Khaild Air Base, air-evac'd to Northrup's contract hospital in Athens, Greece, and finally to the U.S. Air Force Medical Center Weisbeden, Germany. The discharge diagnosis was Ulcerated Colitis.

I returned to Gainesville, FL following my assignment with Northrup to be with my biological daughter. I wasn't able to find employment or bond with my daughter. I gave away all our furniture and household belongings to some religious group and moved to London, KY.

While in London, I worked for approximately one month as a Security Consultant in Nassau, Bahamas followed by a ninety day employment as Kentucky Supervisor for the Pony Express Courier Corporation. The consultant assignment was successful; however, I learned I was not suited for the position with Pony Express. I resigned.

From Pony Express, my wife, son and I re-located to Khamis Mushayt, Saudi Arabia for the first employment stint with

McDonnell Douglas Services.

After two years, the three of us moved to Mesa, Arizona. My wife went her way (divorce) and my son ran away. However, I did find employment with the U.S. Army Military Entrance Processing Station for two different employment periods. One as a Travel Clerk and Testing Clerk.

Following the last employment assignment in Saudi Arabia (which I will address in more detail later.), I was unable to find employment in the metro-Phoenix area. However, I was able to find season employment at the Grand Teton Lodge, WY prior to becoming homeless.

After my contract terminated with the lodge, I moved to Detroit, MI to stay with an aunt and be with my son.

After a period of unemployment, I found work with the Canteen Service at the Veterans Medical Center, Allen Park, MI. Almost, immediately, I was accepted by the Department of Veterans Affairs as a Mail Clerk.

At the end of 1992, I submitted documentation for a transfer to the Louisville, KY Veterans Administration Medical Center as a Medical Clerk. In the first quarter of 1998, the Department of Veterans Affairs retired me with a diagnosis of Post Traumatic Stress Disorder.

I returned to Laurel County, KY, my place of birth, in 2001. My 35 years of Federal Government, Federal Government Contract Employment, and short civilian employment revealed to me there those individuals that sell out their country, their families and their countrymen for money and the worship of a fabricated GOD. Nowhere is dishonor and treason more prevalent than in both Houses of the United States Congress and the Chief Executive Office of the United States Government.

RELIGION

THE ONLY THREAT TO THE UNITED STATES OF AMERICA

Definitions, per Reader's Digest Oxford Complete Word Finder, Copyright 1996: (1) Religion: the belief in a superhuman controlling power, especially, in a personal God or gods entitled to obedience and worship. (2) Freedom of Religion: the right to follow whatever religion one chooses. (3) Constitution: the body of fundamental laws, principles, or established precedents according to which a nation, state, or other organizations is acknowledged to be governed. (4) Republic: a nation in which supreme power is held by the people or their elected representatives or by an elected or nominated president, not a monarch. (5) President: the elected head of a republican government.

Title definition opinion: The President of the United States has the title of Commander In Chief of the U.S. Military. However, the title is very misleading because of the news pundits and fabricators at the White House in administrations past.

Yes, the US Constitution identifies the President as Commander-in-Chief of US Forces. However, in no sense of the imagination was the President or the Vice President granted the authority by the nation's founders to tell the Generals how to conduct a war. Moreover, there is not way in hell that a Vice President had the authority to conduct air defense exercises and order US military resources to deploy or stand down. Not even the President has such an authority.

The President is an important figure in the promotion and assignments of Flag Officers. More important, the dictates of the U.S. Constitution grants the authority for the President to conduct foreign policy. Congress has an oversight authority but foreign policy remains with the President. If Congress objects then, again per the Constitution, with a majority they may defeat the President plans.

Besides the controversy regarding the Presidents role as Commander In Chief of the Armed Forces is that of the presidential candidates religion (in my life time). To this end, religion arose in Presidential Candidate John F. Kennedy's campaign. Mr. Kennedy, in one of his famous speeches, assured the nation that his administration would govern from the provisions of the US Constitution, not Papal Directives. The Roman Catholic Pope would have no say in the governing of the American people.

Moreover, continuing with the American Presidency and religion, while reading the Lexington Herald-Leader newspaper, the morning of June 11, 2011, I came an article address both the presidency and religion. The title of the article was: "Religion and the race for president" with a sub-title: "Survey about faith of candidates suggests added hurdles for Mormons."

Regarding the article, I will only quote the survey results: "Eighty -three percent said they were entirely or somewhat comfortable with Roman Catholics, 80 percent with Jews, 67 percent with evangelical Christians, and 60 percent with Mormons."

"But 36 percent said were uncomfortable with Mormons. Only

atheists and Muslims drew higher discomfort ratings."

"In addition, 45 percent said they had favorable opinions of the Mormon religion - with 32 percent saying their views were unfavorable."

Returning my brainwashing, religious brainwashing began before birth in my mother's womb. During my school years, I spent more time in some type of religious training than I did in school.

One of my earliest memories were the summer's I sent at an aunt's house where my cousins and I attended Bible School. The biblical teachers taught us from the Old Testament. We learned of the Hebrew (Arabs) and their struggle against their fellow Arabs.

The stories of Abraham, King David, Noah's Flood, Noah's Ark, Hebrews in Egypt, Moses, the Ten Commandments, Sodom & Gomorrah, Samson & Delilah, the Tower of Babel, the Roman occupiers, the Opening of the Red Sea, etc., etc. were emphasized throughout the summers. Never was their like stories of the other Arabs living in Palestine and present day Iraq.

Our Bible School, Sunday School, and the hundreds, if not thousands, of sermons never once identified the Islam religion. The teachings and sermons were about the Judeo-Christian religions. Not until I was employed in the Middle East did I learn of Islam.

Moreover, to this date, I have never heard a clergymen say that the God of Abraham is the God of the worshipers of Judaism, Christianity, and Islam. The religious entity's name is different but Abraham is the source of their belief.

Beginning with my high school years, my father had purchased a set of World Book Encyclopedia which I used to read sitting in a tree behind our home. At school, during study hall, I would read National Geographic and other magazines that enlightened one to the international community. Also, at home, my mother allowed me to subscribe to magazines and build models (airplanes, ships, automobiles, etc.) that enhanced my education.

What these reading hours taught me was that what I taught in the religious brainwashing sessions were untrue.

Let us look at Abraham the Hebrew. This alleged individual was an Arab from a civilized community of UR, present day Iraq. He, according to Old Testament, was the leader of a large clan and wealthy. Because of drought in Ur, he and his clan traveled into Canaan (Palestine) seeking water and food for his livestock and clan members. (How Abraham became justifiable known as Abraham the Hebrew is troubling to me. He was an Arab. The Hebrews were a name designated for a different ethnic group of Arabs.)

The clan's travel into Palestine was not uncommon as the population of the immediate region was Arab; whereas, entry into another region, his clan would not be foreign. Also, from the Old Testament, we learned, the Hebrew Arabs would travel into Egypt or any other land space at will. They (Hebrew) acknowledged no land space boundaries. I suppose this activity where the name of a parasite plant called Wandering Jew originated.)

The alleged placement of a son on an altar to offer as an appeasement to their religious entity was not uncommon. However, later in history, an Arab leader made it illegal to kill a child for whatever the purpose.

Now to Noah's Ark and Flood.

Yes, indeed there were floods in region but not due to a religious entity opening the windows in the heavens to release the rain.

No, there was no Noah's Ark. For crying out loud no individual family could have built such as vessel or gather two of each animal species in the world. Of course, someone will say, Noah's religious entity assisted in the building and gathering of the animals. Please, a number of civilizations from the region had a similar story but used different vessels and the reasons for the flood.

Keeping with the water façade, the separation of the Red Sea is absurd. There may have been a body of water that disappeared for awhile and then refilled. Not too long back, I read a National Geographic article telling at intervals, one part of the Jordan River would dry and then refill. (Nothing new. Reminds one of Old Faithful in Yellowstone National Park.)

Of note, what religious zealots don't want to accept is that the earth's plates are constantly moving which causes many events to take place. For example, Sodom and Gomorrah were destroyed by an earthquake. (Scientist are predicting Jerusalem will be hit by an earthquake in the very near future. The planet is going to change its physical identity.)

The Ten Commandments is another plagiarized story/event taken from other civilizations. The original published set of laws were set in stone by one of the greatest Kings of Babylonia–Hammurabi.

The alleged Moses and/or Hebrew scribes were knowledgeable of Hammurabi's Laws and used said laws to bring about civility to the Hebrew tribes.

Recently, May 27, 2011, we learned new tombs in a multiple number of pyramids were discovered in Egypt and the Sinai. Egyptian archaeologists believe the tombs belonged to the workers who built the great pyramids, shedding light on how the laborers lived more than 4,000 years ago.

The same article Amihai Mazar, professor at the Institute of Archaeology at the Hebrew University of Jerusalem, stated that myth stemmed from an erroneous claim by former Israeli Menachem Begin, on a visa to Egypt in 1977, that Jews built the pyramids.

"No Jews built anything because Jews didn't exist at the period when the pyramids were built."

On the same date, there was another report pertaining to the Egyptian Pyramids. The main point of the article was that "scientists say pyramids could be concrete. If so, this finding would mean the ancient Egyptians were great materials scientists as well as great civil engineers."

The stories in the Old Testament such as Samson and Delilah were written by Hebrew scribes to emulate stories from Greek and Roman mythology.

The Tower of Babel story is another falsehood written by Hebrew Arab scribes. Yes, there was a Tower of Babel and the base exists to date; however, the intent was not as a stairway to heaven. There were individuals of different races and languages at the tower due to the kingdom being the power of the region. Prosperity and security brings people, regardless of the country, looking for a better way of life. No religious entity changed races nor languages.

Now to Jesus.

Prior to joining the U.S. Air Force, Jesus Christ was taught to be the Son of God. Today, I learned the religious community is calling Jesus God. I suppose Jesus evolved like gossip. The story gets bigger and greater one generation to the next.

Moreover, the Roman Empire has no record of an entity known as Jesus that could walk on water, raise the dead, make wine and bread or return sight to the blind. To this end, if there were a divine person living in Palestine under the administration of the Roman Empire, surely the Romans would have abducted Jesus for the Empire's own purpose. Also, Jesus' nationality was Palestinian. His race Arab.

In a previous paragraph, I identified the three major religions in the United States: Judaism, Christianity and Islam. Now let us take a closer look at these religions.

Judaism was the first of the three to become a power and economic force in Palestine. The religion established clergymen to provide guidance, administer laws, and collect money. Hebrew Arabs were to visit Jerusalem a specified number of times each year (commerce). Judaism difference is that the Hebrew Arabs claim to be God's Chosen People. Their religious entity was/is the God of Abraham.

The second was Christianity which is basically the same as Judaism except, allegedly, one must believe in Jesus Christ before they can enter into the Kingdom of Heaven. Their religious entity - the God of Abraham.

The third, Islam, originated from the Arabian peninsula. In fact, a wealthy Arab Jew, at his death, willed the Prophet Muhammed vast sums of wealth to assist in his ministry. Islam's revision of Judaism and Christians dictates there is only one God and that is Allah. Muslims, like the Hebrew Arabs visit to Jerusalem, are charged with visiting Mecca a number of times during their lifetime.

Beside the religious community quest for power and money, the Holy Roman Empire introduced Christianity to their empire. Constantine 1, the Great, Emperor of the Holy Roman Empire, became a Christian. From his conversion came an order to publish a Bible for the Christians. Going further Constantine 1, ordered Sunday to be the day of worship. These steps enhanced the demise of the Holy Roman Empire.

Hebrew Arabs, Christians, Muslims began to gain power. The

Hebrew Arabs revolted a number of times against their Roman occupiers. They claimed they established two kingdoms, Judea and Samaria within Palestine. Regardless of claims, the Hebrew Arabs never had a sovereign country of their own until May 1948.

Christians brought the Crusades to Jerusalem. Overall the Christians failed.

Muslims conquered a large area of the known world and spread their religion throughout.

King Ferdinand and Queen Isabella defeated the Arabs/Muslims on the Iberian peninsula and deported them to different locations in the international community. Some say the Carolina land space of North America received a number of the Arabs of different religions. Recent readings revealed many of those expelled migrated to Turkey.

Now to North America and eventually the United States of America. To this end, most citizens of the Red States claim the United States was founded as a Christian country. However, these claims are false. The United States was never nor not at the present a Christian nation. Our country's form of Government is a Constitutional Republic.

For a moment, let us reveal what the Christians did in New England during the 1640s. The clergy was the power; whereas, their rulings was the law. This law brought about people being burned at a stake, individuals placed in stocks, Christians being dunked into a pool of water while attached to a chair, and, of course, individuals having to war an "A" on their outer garments to identify themselves as adulterous.

And, in some of the colonies, clergymen were paid from government treasuries. Thomas Jefferson ended the practice of paying clergymen in Virginia which was followed by other governments.

During the John Adams and Thomas Jefferson's Administrations, the United States was engaged with the pirates of the Barbary Coast (Libya). (Sadly, June 7, 2011, our country is still engaged in hostilities with Libya.) A treaty between the United States, approved by the Senate, ending the war between the two countries. The treaty stated the United States was not a Christian Country. (Sometime later, there were attempts to change our country's religious status as stated on the treaty.)

In 1898, the Zionist Movement was started which stated that Hebrew Arabs must have a homeland for themselves. A number of physical locations were considered; however, the British Government issued the Balfour Doctrine. This doctrine stated the Hebrew Arabs would have a home in Palestine. Later a White Paper to the Doctrine re-worded to include a two state solution: Palestine and Israel.

Hundred of thousands of Palestinians were murdered, forced to flee Palestine, and their land and possessions taken from them by the Hebrew Arabs settlers from throughout the international community.

In the United States, during the aggression against the Palestinians, American Hebrew Arabs sold their business, quit their jobs, removed their stock from Wall Street and moved to

Palestine. Their actions enhanced our country's Great Depression plus an attempted coup against President Franklin D. Roosevelt.

At the death of President Roosevelt, Vice President Harry S. Truman, per the U.S. Constitution, assumed the Helm of State.

In May 1948, President Truman, against the advise of his Secretary of State, other cabinet members, most of the state department's career staff and military chiefs, acknowledged to the international community the establishment of the sovereign State of Israel.

Of note, Truman's decision without a doubt was based on his religious brainwashing and his business partner and life long friend, a devote Zionist, Eddie Jacobson.

Within hours of Truman's declaration, Joseph Stalin, the Supreme Leader of the Soviet Union, announced his support for the new state of Israel.

Both Truman and Stalin need the support of their Hebrew Arab (Jews) population. Truman needed Zionist money and Jewish voting bloc to be elected President of the United States for a full four year term which he received. Stalin need Jewish support to ease the domestic turmoil created by the Soviet Union's large Jewish community.

Succeeding Truman was General of the Army Dwight David Eisenhower. President Eisenhower came to the White House during the Korean War and aggressive actions by the Israeli's. France, and Great Britain against the Egyptians. Eisenhower brought both situations to a stalemate. An ending of hostilities between North and South Korea plus the allies of the two warring nations. Israel and her lackey's withdrew to begin aggression another day.

At the end of Eisenhower's Administration, Fidel Castro, Raul Castro, Che' Guevara and thousands of impoverished Cubans rose up against the government of General Fulgencio Batista. (A Cuban Sergeant that made himself General and Dictator of Cuba.)

Regrettably, the Eisenhower Administration has been blamed for the failed Bay of Pigs invasion financed and directed by the U.S. Central Agency. His administration was not. The failure lies at the feet of President John F. Kennedy and Robert Kennedy.

Of note there are several movies about the Cuban Crisis. An older one Havana starring Robert Redford gives one an insight to the wealth, corruption and the poor of Cuba. A more current film, X-Men, the producer and director blend into the story, U.S. missiles on station in Turkey poised to strike the Soviet Union.

In the film, the screenwriters point out that the missiles targeted against the Soviet Union were an immediate threat to the sovereignty of the Soviets. In truth, the missiles were withdrawn from Turkey in accordance with the agreement between the U.S. and the Soviet Union. However, today, June 8, 2011, the U.S. Government and lackey nations are proposing a missile shield be placed against Russia. (I wonder which Zionist dominated President ordered this aggressive act.)

In October 1960, after Castro had overthrown the Batista

Government, Castro nationalized Mafia Casino's and other properties plus outlawed gambling. Also, properties belonging to powerful Jewish families and others were nationalized. The Cuban government became landlords, farmers, cigar manufacturers, etc.

Regarding the nationalization of Jewish property, the Jewish population of southern Florida, New York, California and other Zionist controlled states are responsible for the boycotting of Cuba. The Cuban government or Cuban people did nothing to the United States.

We've already identified one failure of President of John F. Kennedy but failed to identify his Vice President Lyndon B. Johnson. These two individuals continued the treasonous acts of former President Harry S. Truman for which our country has suffered since May 1948.

From documents read, we learned President Kennedy following his election, told the Jewish community it was their money and votes that put him in the White House. I suppose in gratitude, President Kennedy provided Israel with defense missiles and other support which changed the balance of power in the Middle East to favor Israel.

But, wait? Not to be outdone, President Lyndon B. Johnson provided Israel with aggressive military hardware and cover-up of Israel's aggression against U.S. Naval Forces.

In 1967, Israel attacked their Arab neighbors with military hardware, allowed Americans to fight in the Israeli military, and covered for Israel at the United Nations. Unknown to the majority of Americans, the weapons used against the Arabs and American sailors were provided by the United States and France.

A fleet commander on station in nearby waters when learning of the Israeli attack on the USS Liberty ordered the launch of U.S. combat aircraft to support the Liberty. The Johnson administration recalled the aircraft.

On June 8, 2011, the 44th anniversary of the Israel attack on the USS Liberty, I read an OpEdNews article regarding the incident. From the article, we learned a number of distinguished Americans created a Commission to investigate the incident. Members of the Commission were: Admiral Tom Moorer (retired Chief of Naval Operations and Chairman of the Joints Chiefs of Staff), former Judge Advocate General of the US Navy Admiral Merlin Staring, Marine Corps General Raymond G. Davis, and former US Ambassador to Saudi Arabia James Adkins. (I learned of the attack from a Playboy Magazine while stationed in Southeast Asia. In the late 1970s, while stationed in the Philippines, I watch gun camera film of the attack on Filipino National Television.)

The Commission's Report concluded:

"That there is compelling evidence that Israel's attack was a deliberate attempt to destroy an American ship and kill her crew."

"That fearing conflict with Israel, the White House deliberately prevented the US Navy from coming to the defense of USS Liberty by recalling Sixth Fleet military rescue support while the ship was under attack."

"That surviving crew members were threatened with "court -martial, imprisonment or worse if they exposed the truth; and (the survivors) were abandoned by their own government."

"That there has been an official cover-up without precedent in American naval history."

"That a danger to our national security interests exists whenever our elected officials are willing to subordinate American interests to those of a foreign nation."

A few years past, I checked out the book "Six Day War," written by a dual citizenship (American/Israeli) individual named Michael Oren. (The last I heard his name mentioned, he was Israel's Ambassador to the United States.) From Mr. Oren's book, a day before the attack a US ship maker was on the operations planning board as being in international waters but was removed prior to the attack.

Over the years, I've learned Kennedy had good ideals. For example, he wanted to end the massive military support to Israel and terminate the Federal Reserve. He was murdered.

President Lyndon B. Johnson may be credited for easing race relations that President Eisenhower began by signing the 1964 Civil Rights Act. However, I question his logic in visiting eastern Kentucky and establishing a dollar amount to identify poverty levels.

Enter into the White House a born-again religious zealot, President Jimmy Carter. This man's belief in the God of

Abraham cost the United States taxpayers billions of dollars annually. These expenditures are due to the Camp David Accords signed by President Sadat of Egypt and Prime Minister Begin of Israel for Israel to return the Sinai Desert to Egypt.

Not only have the taxpayers suffered through the illegal expenditures of funds but two hundred plus military personnel killed during a rotation of forces to secure the Sinai Desert. The two hundred plus at Gander, Canada increasing every year. Your sons and daughters are dying because of a non-existing God.

Being truthful, President Carter's program for alternate energy and the solar panels placed on the White House if allowed to proceed/remain, our country would most likely would be free from fossil fuels. President Reagan cancelled Carter's programs and had the solar panels removed.

And, again on the negative side. President Carter attempted to play the leader of the world in human rights which often caused life long friends to question their association with the United States.

Carter's friendship with the Shah of Iran resulted in the employees of the Tehran U.S. Embassy being taken hostage toward the end of this term in office. However, an even more troublesome misadventure occurred when the North Koreans captured the United States Ship Pueblo and held American sailors hostage.

President Carter authorized and Congress agreed to return the Panama Canal Zone to the government of Panama.

With regards to Carter's one term in office, we read communications regularly about Reagan's Election Team and George W. Bush's illegal activities to influence American Jewish and Israeli communities to assure the defeat of President Jimmy Carter.

From reading documents that are being published regularly, we find, in the opinions of many, that Ronald W. Reagan was a made man by the religious community - Reverend Jerry Falwell the 700 Club minister Pat Robertson.

President Ronald W. Reagan and former President Harry S. Truman probably are responsible for the greatest crimes by a Presidential Administration against the American people in our country's history.

Reagan and, before him, President Carter used the power of the United States to bring millions of Soviet Jews to the United States, Israel and Germany. (These three countries paid better benefits to the Jews.)

Reagan ordered the U.S. military to ferry Jews from Ethiopia to Israel.

Congress, with Reagan's signature, provided Israel with funds to build an aircraft industry in competition with U.S. Aircraft Manufacturers.

Reagan authorized a U.S. Naval Fleet to support Great Britain's War in the Falklands.

Reagan ordered a U.S. Marine Expeditionary Force to Lebanon

to support the Israeli invasion of Lebanon. Hundreds of Marines and U.S. Embassy personnel were killed and injured.

Reagan order the military to remove Cuban forces and the Cuban designated leader of Grenada.

Regarding Reagan, there isn't enough space to reveal the damage Reagan and George Herbert Walker Bush did to this great nation.

Vice President Bush became President of the United States of America. During Bush's term, he removed U.S. Forces from Somalia. Ordered the invasion of Panama to remove that country's leader the U.S. made and supported for years.

Supposedly, the greatest accomplishment during President Bush's administration was the forced removal of Iraqi military forces from Kuwait. (Without a doubt, the U.S. government prompted Iraq's invasion of Kuwait. Lies, lies, lies.)

President Bush's Secretary of State James Baker offended the Israeli Government and Zionist by now approving loan guarantees to build more illegal settlements in Palestine. Bush lost reelection.

Enter President William Jefferson Clinton from the state of Arkansas and Vice President Albert Gore from the state of Tennessee. Clinton's administration brought into the international community of nations, the country of Kosovo. (Oh, I should mention the fossil fuel reserves Kosovo possess.)

Clinton ordered the military into Somalia on a humanitarian

mission. However, anyone knows anything about the U.S. State Department and Department of Defense knows the end results of humanitarian deployments - deaths, wounds, loss of international prestige and expenditures of much need dollars in the United States.

In 1998, the Congress of the United States wrote the Iraq Resolution Act and President Clinton signed the Act. The Act funded and ordered President Clinton to remove President Saddam Hussein as Iraq's Head of State.

President Clinton didn't dispatch U.S. Forces to remove Saddam Hussein. However, he did order a number of missile and air strikes at Iraq.

President Clinton was impeached by the U.S. House of Representatives but the U.S. Senate did not remove him from office. I've wondered if Clinton's impeachment was due to his refusal to invade Iraq and remove Saddam Hussein. Monica was a sidebar.

Our next President of the United States was put in office by the Supreme Court of the United States of America - George Walker Bush. Bush's Vice President was Richard Cheney.

Regarding Bush and Cheney, I have only thre entry's.

The first is Bush and Cheney were involved in some manner in the aerial assault on the United States on September 11, 2001. In my mind, the attack was a prelude to a coup attempt similar to the one President Bush's grandfather, Prescott Bush, and other Wall Street Bankers including old money families.

Prescott Bush's attempt failed as did President George Walker Bush.

The second, President Bush ordered the invasion of Afghanistan to assure U.S. Forces would secure the country for the installation of a 7.6 billion gas and oil pipeline.

The third, President Bush ordered the invasion of Iraq as a religious crusade to remove Saddam Hussein and war against the religion of Islam. (A number news pundits and/or heads of state, reported President stated God told him to invade Iraq.)

In my opinion, which many former members of Congress and a former President agrees, is that no American can be elected to any national office unless he or she pledges to support the state of Israel ahead of the people of the United States and our Republic.

Moreover, the Vice President of the United States, Joseph Biden, Web Site declares the Vice President is a Zionist. Senator Charles Schumer of New York recently stated that his name meant Guardian and that he was a Guardian for Israel. I am an American and you may worship or not worship a God or gods of your choice; however, in my opinion, Zionist should be charged with subversion against the United States of America.

The United States is physical land, air, and water space. Our country are coordinates on the planet's globe. The God of Abraham is a fabricated entity just as Santa Claus, Mickey Mouse, etc.

US military personnel swore an oath to defend this great nation against a physical enemy. We are not a Crusading Army. The Joints Chiefs of Staff should remind Congress of the military's purpose and say no to any further military deployments to appease US corporations or the State of Israel.

The failure of Congress, the President, and the Joint Chiefs of Staff, to remove religion from the government of the United States, our country will fall becoming a theocracy which will results in a civil war. However, the final civil war will between religions.

Regrettably, Congress has allowed Jewish Rabbis to hold special courts for Jews. This isn't right. We all are under the dictates of the U.S. Constitution, not a fabricated book to worship a non-existing religious entity. We Americans do not need a superior entity for security and prosperity. We only need our countrymen - Americans.

RELIGIOUS SUBVERSION

The illustration of Uncle Sam, along with a group of individuals carrying knives and the Holy Bible, has been a source of concern, by the religious community, since I had the illustration drawn for inclusion into my book "Enough is Enough."

I have no malice against anyone worshiping whatever entity he or she chooses. Americans have the right per the 1st Amendment of the United States Constitution. Americans also have the right not to believe in an unseen, unheard, non-physical entity, religious or not.

I do have deep concerns about the religious community when the followers of religion place their loyalty with the Supreme Being or God ahead of the United States of America.

In Sunday's, July 24, 2011, Lexington Herald-Leader Newspaper were two articles referencing religion in the OPINION/IDEAS Section.

One titled "WE HAVE GODS BECAUSE WE NEED THEM," subtitle "Faith in the supernatural is another adaptation to help mankind survive." The article was co-authored by Anderson Thompson, a psychiatrist at the University of Virginia. Clare Aukofer is a medical writer.

The following are quotes of the last two paragraphs:

"We can be better as a species if we recognize religion as a man-made construct. We owe it to ourselves to at least consider the real roots of religious beliefs, so we can deal with life as it is, taking advantage of perhaps our mind's greatest adaptation: our ability to reason."

"Imagine that."

The second was a crude satire, his words, with the title "Lying about why Commandments posted is a sin," written by Attorney at Law and contributing columnist, Mr. Larry Webster.

What was most interesting in his column, in my opinion, was in relationship to bearing false witness. For example, this would be like swearing in court, the purpose of posting the Ten Commandments in a public facility was for reason other than religion.

Returning to the subject.

While researching chapters in this book, I came across the words of an extremely interesting person - Mr. Benjamin Freedman (Friedman).

The research reveals Mr. Freedman said in 1961, Washington, (paraphrasing): He was a millionaire insider in international Zionist Organizations, friend of 4 US Presidents, and also part of the 117 man strong Zionist delegates at the signing of the Treaty of Versailles in 1919.

For the non-history person, the Treaty of Versailles was where Germany was forced into bankruptcy to Zionist bank lords and social chaos in Germany.

Research further revealed from Mr. Freedman's file. "Two years into World War I, Germany was winning the war; whereas money changers offered Britain and France a negotiated peace deal.

German Zionist groups seeing the opportunity made a deal with Britain to get the United States into the war if Britain promised to give Zionist - Palestine.

Britain acknowledged deal by publishing the Balfour Declaration.

I am awaiting the Laurel County Library to provide me a copy of a book "Behind the Balfour Declaration," "Britain's great war pledge to Lord Rothschild, written by Mr. Robert John. Hopefully, this book will finally put my mind to rest regarding US involvement in World War I and World War II. The two wars go together.

In Kentucky's 5th US Congressional District, which Laurel County is one of 29 counties, the majority of the district's population have never heard of the Balfour Declaration or the British Mandate. However, on any given day throughout the district, you may hear individuals using God's name in their conversation regardless of the subject.

Southeastern and Eastern Kentuckians have been brainwashed from inception in the womb and every day of their lives thereafter, that the God of Abraham exists and it is their responsibility to support the Socialist Country of Israel.

In Washington, DC, the Vice President of the United States of America, Joseph Biden, according to his campaign web site is a declared Zionist. Members of the US House of Representative and US Senate have dual citizenship - US and Israel. Those that do not, will not vote for the United States ahead of Israel for they know they will not be reelected.

Recently, Senator Charles Schumer, New York State, in an interview with a radio reporter stated his name meant Guardian;

whereas, he was a Guardian of Israel.

I am a disabled Air Force Master Sergeant that does not care what religious entity you worship or do not worship. I do take exception, when you place your loyalty to a Supreme Being or God ahead of the United States of America.

Please vote in 2012 and 2014, we must return our country to the dictates of the Declaration of Independence and the US Constitution. To do so, would end the illegal wars and the fiscal failure now being address by Congress and the President of the United States of America.

I AM AN ATHEIST

AS AN AMERICAN, I DO NOT HAVE TO BELIEVE IN A SUPERIOR ENTITY

As I have written and verbally addressed since 2002, based on administrative research, being present in Saudi Arabia and Egypt plus the results of two separate DNA test, Father's Ancestry and Father's Chromosome, I can not believe in a superior entity.

As an American, the Declaration of Independence and the U.S. Constitution are the foundations of the United States Republic. The United States has latitude and longitude coordinates as part of the North American land mass. Our country has fertile flat lands, mountains, deserts, rivers, lakes, wildlife, fish, individuals from every race, ethnic group, or religion, and every form of matter needed for life, liberty and the pursuit of happiness.

The Torah plus accompanying documents, Bible, and the Koran are fiction. There were publications written to undermine their fellow human beings. The made claims as to their own superiority above their fellow man and that their God was the supreme religious entity.

As a southeastern Kentuckian, my vocabulary is limited in explaining the stress and frustration I have encountered since childhood, especially since 2002, regarding religion. In this light, I found an article "Theistic Bigotry: The Reality of Denying Fantasy" at OpEdNews.com, that defines my religious association in a Zionist Commonwealth. The author was: Mr. Frank Ranelli.

"While religionists in the U.S. continue to enjoy a privileged status for their unfounded beliefs, unbelievers face increasing acts of life-altering prejudice and discrimination by America's pious."

"Atheist are, by every metric, measured in polls, still the most distrusted and maligned minority, which now makes up a healthy 10.7% of the U.S. populace. And the "crime" against society atheists commit with each breath —a lack of belief in the supernatural due to an overwhelming lack of evidence. Often, this victimless thought crime carries harsh punitive consequences to the nonbeliever – being ostracized and harangued by family and friends, loss of career, immovable bulwarks blocking entrance to public office, jeers, sneers, and occasionally even reprisals of violence." (1)

"Author Sam Harris, in his October 2005 article, "There is No God (And You Know It)," (2) perhaps encapsulates this senseless absurdity of theistic bigotry best: "Atheism is not a philosophy; it is not even a view of the world; it is simply a refusal to deny the obvious. Atheism is nothing more than the noises reasonable people make when in the presence of religious dogma; however, that places the atheist at the margins of society. The atheist, by merely being in touch with reality, appears shamefully out of touch with the fantasy life of his neighbors.""

"Indeed, when the courage to exclaim openly one's confirmation of mere reality leads to palpable prejudice -- rather than to stay hidden in the shadows of ancient dogma for societal acceptance, then one thing become abundantly clear: faith needs more criticism and scrutiny, not less."

Above all, I am American. You can worship your left big toe as your superior entity, I do not care. But, please, do not attempt to impose your toe on me or in the administration of the government of the United States of America.

COMMONWEALTH OF KENTUCKY NULL AND VOID

RELIGON, WELFARE, DRUGS, AND SPORTS DESTROY A PEOPLE

Prior to 1965, the people of the Commonwealth residing in Kentucky's 5th U.S. Congressional District were farmers, traders, coal miners, bootleggers, and prayed to the God of Abraham at least three times per day. Equally important, they had inherent knowledge how to repair, build, renovate just about anything. Hay bailing wire, twine, and glue kept equipment operational which, in-turn, produced food stuff for both humans and animals.

Yes, without a doubt, most citizens lived below the living standards of most of the nation and, for sure, Kentucky's city dwellers.

Sadly, racism, family history and pride, love of fox hunting, fishing, and hunting in general, plus their dedication to either the Democrat or Republican Party kept many families from assimilating. In some counties, failure to assimilate still exists as does racism.

In 1965, President Lyndon Baines Johnson came to eastern Kentucky followed by others such politicians as Robert Kennedy. Allegedly, their goal was to see how Americans could be living in such poverty unlike most of the industrial northern states. Vast fortunes were coming from the mining industry. However, as Kentuckians from the region know, Giant Corporations and Frankfort were the enriched, not the average citizen of the 5th Congressional District.

From Johnson's visit came a formulated dollar amount to inform our countrymen if they were below or above the new demeaning label - POVERTY.

Without a doubt the people of the region needed to be upgraded to the benefits available from their American citizenship. (As children we were all taught of the American Dream. Americans were wealthy, healthy, and had undisputed freedoms. None of the three are true then or now.)

Yes, without a doubt, any American regardless of race, gender, sexual preference, and religion can advance in our country. However, you must have initiative that entails discipline, seeking an education, questioning established rule and regulations, and the will to leave your homestead to another location that will provide you the alleged American Dream.

For myself, I knew that I could not attain the goals that I had established for myself in Kentucky plus discord with my stepfather prompted me to join the United States Air Force. The next 35 years under primarily the employment umbrella of the federal government, I was able to meet all but one of my many goals.

I returned to my hometown, London, KY, in 2001. However, from 1993 to 2001, I lived and worked in the City of Louisville, KY. In Louisville, we witnessed generation after generation residing in government Section Eight Housing or Government housing projects. The people in the rental assistance or housing projects, for the most part, were on food stamps, received monthly payments from the government, were provided Medicaid or Medicare Cards and heating and air conditioning bill payments.

There were others that had served in the military for a short period; whereas, they received a Non-Service Connected Pension and gratis health care at the Louisville Veterans Affairs Medical Center. These individuals lived better than the average men and women residing in Louisville and the suburbs. Of course, they were the minority instead of the majority.

From what I had witnessed and learned in Louisville and working at the Louisville Veterans Administration Medical Center, when I returned to London, I became interested in going to Washington and attempt to return our government to the principles of the Declaration of Independence and the dictates of the United States Constitution.

Having been gone for 35 years and my mother dead, I had

no base of support. Yes, I had an extremely large family that remain in London and Laurel County. However, I was, I suppose the Black Sheep, as I did not conform with the religious teachings established over the years of my absence. They were, in my opinion, stronger than the day I departed on September 30, 1960.

For those not familiar, the 5th US Congressional District assigned to Laurel County is one of 29 counties in south and southeastern Kentucky. The U.S. House of Representatives member for more than 20 years is and has been the Honorable Harold Rogers (R-KY). The Congressman's Kentucky's primary office is in Somerset, KY.

In my opinion, the primary reason Congressman Rogers has remained in Congress so long is that he brings home federal dollars in all shapes and sizes to the district. He is, without a doubt, a Congressman of the people instead of the U.S. Constitution. I suspect in some way in his tenure, he has assisted a member of families at one time or another throughout his district. He certainly assisted me with the Department of Veterans Affairs.

Moreover, in my opinion, Congressman Rogers' answers to questions sent to him are answered primarily with the standardized response originated by the Republican Party. We disagree on the Republican Party's unquestionable support for the Socialist State of Israel. Another disagreement is the largest problem in our state, the education of our citizens to the point they will become productive citizens.

Sadly, in the 5th Congressional District, we have citizens that are racist. Equally disturbing, the lack of an education curriculum that enforces science, true world history, social studies, and mandatory classes in to all areas envisioned by the founders of this great nation. Religious studies should be scrutinized by both federal and state governments to eliminate the untruths and racist messages. (You can worship your left big toe because the 1st Amendment of the U.S. Constitution guarantees your right but do not attempt to interject your toe into government affairs or knock on my door.) Without knowledge of the past, as someone said, we are doomed to repeat it.

Now let us address the Kentucky's State Government.

The November 2011, Kentucky's Governor's Race reveals individuals, in my opinion, that emphasize their religious affiliation because they know the will receive votes because of their alleged religion. For example, one of Governor Steve Beshear's political campaign adds state my father and grandfather were ministers. In a republic, who cares. His guidance comes from Kentucky's and the US Constitution, not the Bible, Torah, or Koran.

Governor Beshear's political rival in the Governor's Race is Kentucky State Senate President David Williams. To this end, in June 11, 2001, Lexington Herald-Leader newspaper, in a Letter to the Editor, a Mr. David Zimmerman wrote "The rights of our gay and Lesbian family members will not be realized without straight allies standing up against bigotry. That bigotry beats in the heart of Kentucky Senate President David Williams."

Equally disturbing, in my opinion, Senate President William's running mate is Kentucky Agriculture Director as been in the news a lot lately due to his management of the Agriculture's Division of state government. But, wait, during his college days at the University of Kentucky, he was a basketball star.

Digressing a bit, the November 2010, US Senator's Race revealed, in my opinion, candidate Rand Paul candidacy was enhanced a great deal by the media's constant reporting of Rand Paul's religious beliefs by Senatorial Candidate Attorney General Jack Conway.

Regarding the sub subjects of this chapter, let me address a religious factor that is denying the people of Kentucky employment, approval to replace Kentucky's former major crop, in my lifetime, with the Industrial Hemp Plant.

Someone just asked, what does the Industrial Hemp Plant have to do with religion. The answer is simple, the clergymen can't or want accept the fact that Industrial Hemp is not Marijuana. You can't get high on Industrial Hemp.

Of note, I have never used Marijuana but I know people that did and do. Furthermore, if the sale of alcoholic drinks are legal to sell then so should Marijuana. Kentucky needs revenue, so sell licenses to grow Marijuana for medical purposes and tax the sale of the marijuana from the vendor. Marijuana's side effects, to my understanding, aren't as alcohol and tobacco.

Since 2002, I have written a number of letters to the newspapers, members of Congress and anyone else that I felt could return Industrial Hemp to Kentucky's farmlands. So, instead of using my words to enlighten the use of Industrial Hemp, I will quote selective paragraphs of Mr. Rand Clifford's news release titled "Hemp, The Great Green Hope" printed June 11, 2011 at OpEdNews.Com.

HEMP, THE GREAT GREEN HOPE

"It has something to do with something called marijuana. I believe it is a narcotic of some kind."

"So said congressman Rayburn to congressman Snell's question: "What is the bill about?""

"That was way back in the summer of 1937, when congress was being asked to essentially outlaw a drug they knew nothing about, marijuana. But, realistically, marijuana had little to do with it. The real issue was non-drug Industrial Hemp."

"Industrialists were like scarab beetles, rolling around this giant ball of profit protection, and they ran right over the domestic hemp industry. Hemp presented way too much competition, too much threat to entrenched and entrenching profits. Took a pretty big ball of dung, but the scarabs rolled it expertly, professionals. Except for several years of heavy production during WWII, under the feds' "Hemp for Victory" campaign-- which told the truth about hemp and helped us win the war -- note a single acre of hemp has been legally grown in America since 1937. Seventy-four years and counting. That was one enormous ball of dung. The entire hemp-prohibition infamy could be called DUNG DEAL, especially as related to the common good."

"Hemp has taught us many things about how power works in America, and our education continues. Hemp's usefulness is truly remarkable; food, fuel, fiber, paper, plastics--using modern technology, hemp offers an estimated 25,000 natural products. Hemp needs no petrochemical fertilizer, pesticides, herbicides, or fungicides, and is actually beneficial to the soil. Hemp is nature's premier powerhouse for converting sunshine and water (and carbon dioxide while breathing out oxygen) into an astonishing range of superior, eco-friendly products. Perhaps one of the worst things about hemp is that, for the bulk of our perception -managed population, it sounds too good to be true. Well, for about the last 12,000 years hemp has proved true--yet for the last seventy-four years in America, growing hemp has been a crime. THAT'S THE REAL CRIME."

"The U.S. Hemp Industry is currently ringing up $400 million in annual retail sales--all of it on IMPORTED raw materials! The number of good, non-transferable (cannot be "off-shored") jobs hemp prohibition costs us is shameful. We need solid jobs. We need to create value. Other economic benefits of hemp, along with the environmental benefits, are all but incalculable."

"In 2005, republican representative from Texas Ron Paul was chief sponsor of the "Industrial Hemp Farming Act of 2005." The bill would have allowed farmers to grow Industrial Hemp--non-drug varieties of cannabis, differentiating between cannabis strains and setting limits on the amount of psychoactive THC allowed. No, for the environment, the economy, the common good--for everything that deserves a future, that sounded too good to be true."

"Ron Paul tried again in 2007, 2009 and on May 12, introduced the "Industrial Hemp Farming Act of 2011." This time Ron Paul has twenty-two co-sponsors--and that's where differences appear in the way democrats and republicans regard the common good; twenty of the co-sponsors are democrat, two of them republicans. It is the most co-sponsors Ron Paul has attracted so far."

Following the typing of this chapter, I called or wrote every US Congressional delegate representing Kentucky in the Congress of the United States. Stay tuned.

Another ideal of mine which does not fit in to the survival of our state and nation is legalized Gambling. We already have race tracks and the lottery why not take another step forward.

My proposal would be for the State of Kentucky to build a resort at Levi Jackson State Park, London, Kentucky. The resort would offer the same gambling as the rivers boats around the nation or at Las Vegas. Besides the gambling, vendors could establish hunting and fishing adventures. The project would allow Kentucky to receive gambling and other monies now diverted to other states.

Equally important to the location is the fact that London has, I was told, the fifth best airport in the State of Kentucky. The airport coupled with the fact Interstate 75 and the future Interstate 66 run through London.

From London tourist could travel to Dolly Wood, the Grand Ole Opry, the Kentucky Derby, Kentucky's new speedway and the many other recreational facilities in the Commonwealth. Vacations in London would be cheaper and better than Louisville or Lexington.

Returning to the sub topics.

Growing up on Hwy 363, in the 1950s, life was austere; however, my mother raised two gardens and purchased day old bread and pastries from a building behind Kerns Bakery. We wore hand me down clothing and attended religious service whenever they were in session. (My mother was a devote Christian.) During one period, my grandmother, Lucy Wilson, was in need of a care taker. To this end, mother, my sister and I traveled in the mountains of eastern Kentucky to find a candidate. This trips occurred several times. My grandmother was her own person in every way. My father eventually placed her in a nursing home.

The trips cited above ended in serving two purposes. The first was for grandmother. The second provided the opportunity to see how other families lived outside of Laurel County. Like my family most were poor but independent.

Of note, during the 1950s, there weren't any welfare programs like there today, I don't believe. Yes, I know the truly needed could receive government cheese, powered milk, beans and other food stuff. However, I don't believe there were free medical or dental clinic. (When I joined the air force, I had never been to a dentist. When I reached my first permanent party base, I spent a lot of time in the base dentistry.) The people worked either on their own farms or hired out to other farmers to cut tobacco, haul hay, and other farm labor jobs. We, the people of Kentucky's 5th Congressional District may have been poor but we lived without federal or state assistance, in more instances than the people do today.

I don't know who to be angry at the government or those

Kentuckians that misuse the federal and state assistance program. My goodness, there is such much fraud in the community colleges, giving birth to children for money, and the list goes on and on. On the other hand, I know the taxpayers would be better off if our federal government re-introduced some of the programs that the President Franklin D. Roosevelt initiated during the great depression. (Regardless of what our government call these drastic times, we are in a depression.)

Look at the jobs available just to repair our infrastructure. New highways and bridges must be built to handle future automobiles that can drive themselves. President Obama wants to re-establish the railroad industry to the point that surpasses our country's westward movement. Kentucky has outstanding waterways where investments could make the rivers emulate the river days of writer Mark Twain.

All the suggestions and opinions I have offered can be and should be the goal of American politicians. The United States has a physical presence on this planet; whereas, your administrations should be to support the United States of America and the American people. Our form of government is a Constitutional Republic, not a theocracy. Remember not only a Commonwealth belongs to the people, so does our Republic, the United States of America.

I was closing this chapter but today's, June 20, 2011, Lexington Herald-Leader Newspaper's front page story "RELIGON AND POLITICS IN KENTUCKY" seduced me in to elaborating on the front page story.

The referenced story provided a graph of religious representation by the people of Kentucky versus the population of the United States. A short summary was that Kentucky's population is mostly Christian, with a higher percentage of Protestants than the national average.

However, I do not agree with the breakdown of Jewish affiliation as, in my opinion, the majority of the Old Testament Christians in Kentucky are actually covert Jews.

The story was outstanding in pointing that Governor Beshear had identified his father and grandfather as ministers instead of identifying the two were in the funeral home business in his political advertisement. Also, a brief history was provided regarding candidate Paul's Aqua Buddha college prank. (Without a doubt, candidate Conway's misuse of candidate Paul's college prank, cost him the US Senate seat.)

In response to the Herald-Leader's story, I sent the editors an e-mail addressing Article 6, item 3 of the US Constitution which states in part "no religious test shall be required as a Qualification to any office or public trust under the United States." In other words, in my opinion, the subject should never arise.

And, I am sad to report there are eight states (Arkansas, Maryland, Mississippi, North Carolina, Pennsylvania,

South Carolina, Tennessee, Texas) whose State Constitution stipulates "Denial of Office and/or Denial of Witness" for individuals that do not believe in a supreme being. Too me, these laws violate the Declaration of Independence and Article VI of the US Constitution.

Unless federal and state governments start afresh with true Americans in their governing bodies, we will become a Theocracy nation. (One should re-read the 1640s history of the New England Colony Settlements.)

POLITICS

INDEDPENDENT CANDIDATES DENIED DUE PROCESS

Definitions: (1) Democratic Party: one of the two main US political parties, considered to support social reform and strong federal powers. (2) Republican Party: one of the two main US political parties, favoring a lesser degree of central power. (3) Independent Party: not belonging to or supported by a party. (4) Libertarian Party: believer in free will. (5) Constitutional Party: believer in a theocracy government. (based on personal experience.)

While reading the OPINIONS section of Lexington Herald-Leader, June 9, 2011, a Letter to the Editor with the title "Closed primaries take away rights of Kentucky voters." The writer was Mr. Rick Maxfield of Salvisa. Mr. Maxfield, I thank you for this outstanding piece of American history of which I am going to use in this book:

"George Washington despised the ideal of political associations formed in such a way as to pit one group of citizens against another. In his farewell speech in 1796 he said political parties" "serve to organize faction, to give it an artificial and extraordinary force, to put, in the place of the delegated will of the nation, the will of a party, often a small but artful and enterprising minority of the community; and, according to the alternate triumphs of different parties, to make the public administration the mirror of the ill-concerted and incongruous projects of the faction, rather than the organ of consistent and wholesome plans digested by common counsels, and modified by mutual interests."

"Come on Kentucky get with it."

Washington's Farwell Speech is just another example to the wisdom of our founding fathers. What he addressed regarding political parties is alive and well in the state of Kentucky and, most probably, the other states and territories as well.

In 2002 and 2004, I ran against the Honorable Harold Rogers, R-KY, in the Republican Primary in Kentucky's 5th U.S. Congressional District. Everyone said I was wasting my time, that Rogers could not be beaten. However, my goal was not to defeat Mr. Rogers but go to Washington as an American that honors the dictates of the Declaration Independence and the U.S. Constitution.

While traveling and speaking in the 5th District, I informed the population of two major disagreements I had with Congressman Rogers. The first was there was no reason to go to war in Iraq as there were no Weapons of Mass Destruction. The second, I would not be a rubber stamp to the illegal pork projects and welfare abuse in the district.

During my campaign efforts, I did not accept contributions, although offers were made, as I felt to do so would place me in the same category as other individuals seeking public office. To this end, I believe those that accept contributions are bought and paid.

Another factor, I told the truth. A primary truth is that I do not believe religion should have a say in the governing of the American people. Of the 300 plus million Americans, not all believe in a superior being. I am an atheist.

Naturally, I was defeated but made a honorable showing in the polls.

Although defeated, I continue to write letters to members of Congress, the President, and the three major newspapers servicing my immediate local area. After all, the United States of America belongs to the people not the political parties or Wall Street Bankers.

From 2004 forward, our country became a country that emulated Germany prior to World War II. Zionist control the government of the United States as they did in Germany until the German Nationalist Socialist Workers Party assumed the helm of the German Government.

Following World War I, Germany was in debt like the United States is today. International bankers and investors, especially Americans, loaned money and invested heavily in to the rebuilding of Germany. In fact, the German military employed military hardware and vehicles manufactured in Germany by American manufacturers. (I read recently some years after the conclusion of the war, US companies in Germany were paid by the U.S. Government for the war damages inflicted by allied powers during the war.)

The wars in Iraq and Afghanistan are not the results of those countries attacking the United States but the dispatch of U.S.

Forces to assure international investors, especially Zionist, their investments would be protected. For example, the 7.6 billion previously identified to finance gas and oil pipelines through Afghanistan.

In 2010, I became more angry each day with the way the Bush Administration and the members of Congress had/were destroying our great country. So, I decided to run for the U.S. Senate as an Independent Candidate.

However, before I began the administrative tasks, I visited a campaign stop-over at the London Community Center by candidate Rand Paul. I spoke to Mr. Paul regarding U.S. support for Israel. I was not satisfied with his answer and informed that I would be running against him. His aide, Mr. Adams, was more forthcoming.

Again, I did not accept donations or anything that could be construed as expenditures to the $5,000.00 I was allowed to spend during the campaign.

The Secretary of State's Office informed me that I needed 5,000 signatures of registered voters before my name could be placed on Kentucky's ballot. To accomplish this task, I devised a paper for inclusion in a Sunday Herald-Leader newspaper. The paper afforded the reader to sign his or her name plus fold the paper and add stamp. Using this method, I received a few voters signature.

The most signatures received were from the Somerset Community College. However, within the district my lack of religious belief denied me the signatures.

I could have paid multi-thousands of dollars for a professional signature provider for 7,500 signatures. I would not entertain such an ideal not only for the cost but, in my opinion, the practice would be unethical.

With the limited funds, I purchased campaign signs, paid for political inserts and traveled to a number of areas in the state. I even had a political announcement on the screen at Cinema Eight in London. At some locations, I was received well by the public but, at least two locations, a number of individuals walked out due to my telling the truth.

What surprised me most was my reception by Mr. Dean Johnson, Laurel County Clerk. I have always voted for Mr. Johnson, as I believe he is doing an outstanding job as County Clerk; however, it is my opinion, his loyalty lies with his religion, not the dictates of the U.S. Constitution.

Several months following the election and with the re-placement Secretary of State in office, I wrote Secretary of State Walker regarding the election. Along with my correspondence (attached), I made a survey from KY Election Web Site of the votes I received per country and, more important, the number of counties that provided my name on the ballot and/or made available the names of Independent candidates. I was not the only Independent candidate in the different races in Kentucky.

The web site reported that I received 1,214 votes. The disparity between those counties that provided names and/or available information was great. The secretaries letter to me, with attachments revealed my total number of votes were 388. I replied to her letter identifying the error but, to date, no response.

My fellow Americans, the United States of America is the people's country, not a political party. To this end, the Democrats and Republicans act like basketball teams such as the University of Louisville and the University of Kentucky. However, no trophy is awarded, only the fate of the United States is a stake. Don't you think all Americans that meet the legal standards for public office should be allowed equal time campaigning and their names placed on the ballot. (KET refused to allow me to debate the Republican and Democrat candidates.)

I paid my filing fee. I did the documentation.

KENTUCKY STATE FLAG

The motto on Kentucky's State Flag "United We Stand" "Divided We Fall" enforces the Declaration of Independence words that in our country all people are created equal. However, as an American and a citizen of the Commonwealth of Kentucky, I am appalled by the lack of respect and loyalty for the United States of America.

As Americans and Kentuckians, we have responsibilities to this great nation. One of the major responsibilities is to register and then vote whenever an election is announced.

In my hometown, people have told me they don't vote because if they register, then they may be called for Jury Duty. This one example reveals why voter turn-out is in the 40% bracket.

Regarding Jury Duty, the lady that spoke the words, in my opinion, doesn't understand or doesn't care that individuals in earlier civilizations died to make a jury trial possible. However, I do understand her frustration as our country's Attorney General and members of Congress are dividing the people with their legal attacks against individuals whose religion is Islam.

Moreover, the actions of the Attorney General's Office and the Congress of the United States are taking our country in to a steady descent to another War Between the States. However, the cause of this war will be the belief in the fabricated God of Abraham.

If someone actually bought this book, especially from Kentucky 5th US Congressional District, they are upset by words about a fabricated God. Be angry if you want but, for the record, the United States is a Constitutional Republic. The presence of the United States is established by latitude and longitude coordinates on a map of North America. She is in the present.

As Americans, you have responsibilities.

TREY GRAYSON
SECRETARY OF STATE

OFFICE OF THE SECRETARY OF STATE

ELECTION DIVISION
SUITE 148, STATE CAPITOL
700 CAPITAL AVENUE
FRANKFORT, KY 40601-3493
(502) 564-3490
FAX (502) 564-2476
WEBSITE: www.sos.ky.gov

TO: 2010 Write-In Candidates for the General Election

FROM: Trey Grayson
        Secretary of State

RE: **Write-In Candidate Ballot Access Provisions**

To avoid any delay in the proper filing of the Declaration of Intent to be a Write-In candidate filing form for candidates required to file with the Secretary of State, the following is provided.

Earliest date to affix signatures on intent	November 4, 2009
Earliest date to file intent	November 4, 2009
Latest date to file Declaration of Intent to be a Write-In Candidate (4:00 p.m., local time)	October 22, 2010

1. Complete **all applicable** blanks on the declaration of intent to be a write-in candidate.

2. All copies of the Appointment of Campaign Treasurer and Optional Request for Reporting Exemption should accompany the Declaration of Intent to be a Write-In Candidate form. The Secretary of State will make distribution of all copies. **(Not applicable to Federal Candidates who must register with the Federal Election Commission.)**

3. A copy of KRS 117.265, and a chart providing candidate qualifications and filing fees is enclosed. (Checks should be payable to the Kentucky State Treasurer).

The Registry of Election Finance requests that candidates seeking information relating to campaign finance and any reporting forms for campaign contributions and expenditures, download the required reporting forms and a book titled Guide to Campaign Finance from their website, http://www.kref.ky.gov or candidates may directly contact the Registry of Election Finance by calling 502-573-2226.

The Declaration of Intent to be a Write-In Candidate filing form **must** be received in proper form and may be filed in person or by mail, but **must** be received on or before the fourth Friday in October preceding the date of the regular election, (October 22, 2010) 4:00 p.m., local time in the Office of the Secretary of State, Room 148, State Capitol, Frankfort, KY 40601-3493.

KentuckyUnbridledSpirit.com

Equal Opportunity Employer M/F/D

COMMONWEALTH OF KENTUCKY

OFFICE OF THE SECRETARY OF STATE

TREY GRAYSON
SECRETARY OF STATE

ELECTION DIVISION
SUITE 148, STATE CAPITOL
700 CAPITAL AVENUE
FRANKFORT, KY 40601-3493
(502) 564-3490
FAX (502) 564-5687
WEBSITE: www.sos.ky.gov

June 16, 2010

Billy Ray Wilson
209 Autumn Drive
London, KY 40744-7071

Dear Mr. Wilson:

We are in receipt of your letter dated June 13, 2010 regarding filing as an independent candidate for United States Senator. Please be advised KRS 118.315 (2), (copy attached) requires "A petition of nomination for a state officer, or any officer for whom all the electors of the state are entitled to vote, shall contain five thousand (5,000) petitioners". We have no authority to waive a statutory requirement.

The only other ballot access provision available is to file a Declaration of Intent to be a Write-In candidate this requires the completing of a document prescribed by the Kentucky State Board of Elections and a filing fee of $50.00 to be filed with the Kentucky Secretary of State by October 22, 2010 by 4:00 p.m. We have enclosed a Declaration of Intent to be a Write-In Candidate and filing instructions should you so choose to file as a write-in candidate.

If we can be of any further assistance, please let us know.

Sincerely,

Mary Sue Helm

Mary Sue Helm
Election Administrator

enclosures

KentuckyUnbridledSpirit.com

An Equal Opportunity Employer M/F/D

69

BILLY RAY WILSON

209 Autumn Drive
London, KY 40744-7071
(606) 862-2847 phone
(606) 330-0124 fax
brwilson04@windstream.net e-mail

The Honorable Lisa Murkowski
United States Senator
709 Hart Senate Building
Washington, DC 20510

Subject: DENIAL OF DUE PROCESS - 2010 SENATE ELECTION

Dear Senator Murkowski:

Congratulations of your re-election to the U.S. Senate and, more important, Alaska's Supreme Court decision regarding Independent Candidates.

As you realize from the address, I am not a citizen of the state of Alaska; however, I am an American. Yes, Kentucky has two U.S. Senators (Senator Mitch McConnell & Senator Rand Paul) but, in my opinion, neither are Americans. They are political prostitutes seeking their own agenda, not the peoples. (Senator McConnell has made Kentucky a better place, however, his position as Republican Leader demeans not only him, the United States Senate, and the American people. Senator Paul is a disgrace to the human race.)

Now to the subject.

In 2010, I sought the office of U.S. Senate, being vacated by Senator Jim Bunning, as an Independent Candidate. First, I attempted to acquire the number of petition signatures required to be on the ballot. However, due to my lack of funds and limited mobility, I had to change to a Write In Candidate. Immediately, I learned of the bias against Independent Candidates.

Digressing a bit. Prior to filing for the position with Kentucky's Election Commission, I met candidate Rand Paul at a London Political Rally. I spoke to the candidate regarding support for the state of Israel. Following his answer, I informed him that I would be running against him as an Independent Candidate. His advisor told me the candidate was afraid to speak of Israel due to political fallout. No integrity. (Senator Paul did make an insincere effort, in my opinion, at arrival in Congress to end support for Israel.) A true Senator and American would have demanded the termination of support. We are a Constitutional Republic, not a theocracy. (I do not know your stand on Israel but, hopefully, you believe our country is the United States and if you are a citizen, then you are an American.)

Madam Senator, it is time to get our house in order. To do so, we must end the aggression against the people of Islam and terminate support for Israel. There is no God nor, as Thomas Jefferson emphasized, Jesus Christ was a preacher/teacher, not a divine person. The United States is supposed to be first.

Returning to the subject. Congress needs to change laws and/or enforce existing laws that all Americans have a legal right, with media coverage and state equality, to seek national or any public office. The United States is our country.

With respect,

Billy Ray Wilson

BILLY RAY WILSON
Disabled Military Veteran of the Illegal Laotian War

Enclosures: Several

Until the high court rules on the petition for review, the justices said all ballots cast by voters who are provided with the list of write-in candidates should be segregated from other ballots.

Murkowski's campaign was pleased with the high court's decision.

"This stay will ensure that Alaskans can continue to get the assistance they're entitled to under law," said her campaign manager, Kevin Sweeney.

The Alaska Democratic Party criticized the state Division of Elections' appeal to the high court.

"What the DOE has done continues to profoundly complicate this election," Party Chairwoman Patti Higgins said. "They are throwing Alaska votes into question by first, providing the list and second, appealing the temporary restraining order."

"We know that the Alaskan Democratic Party and the Alaskan Republican Party have been fighting to make sure that the people of Alaska have a fair and just election, and that has been what Joe has been advocating all along," Miller campaign spokesman Randy DeSoto said.

The regulation referred to in Pfiffner's ruling reads, "Information regarding a write-in candidate may not be discussed, exhibited, or provided at the polling place, or within 200 feet of any entrance to the polling place."

The judge said the Elections Division implemented a new policy despite "surreptitiously," seeking but not receiving required permission do so from the U.S. Department of Justice under the Voting Rights Act of 1965.

He enjoined the Elections Division from allowing election workers and polling place workers to post write-in candidates, to provide a list of write-in candidate names to voters or to verbally provide the names of write-in candidates to voters.

The Alaska Democratic Party sued Monday over the issue and the Republican Party of Alaska joined the lawsuit. The parties claimed the names handed out by election officials would skew voting in favor of write-in candidates.

The Murkowski campaign had intervened in the lawsuit, arguing that election officials have a broad mandate to assist voters and that the desire of voters for assistance in past court cases has trumped state rules.

At a hearing Monday, Assistant Attorney General Margaret Paton-Walsh said lists of write-in names were only intended as voter assistance and were not forms of advocacy. She said other states routinely post such information at polling places.

SIMILAR STORIES:

* Alaska reversal: Court's write-in ruling could aid Murkowski

* Alaska judge's order deals blow to Murkowski's write-in bid

* Dems, GOP join to challenge Alaska's list of write-ins

* Alaska Dems threaten to sue over write-in lists

* Senate race in Alaska is bitter and unpredictable

COMMENTS

Community Publishing Guidelines

1 person liked this.

Add New Comment

Required: Please login below to comment.

June 13, 2010

Commonwealth of Kentucky
Office of the Secretary of State
Attention: Ms. Mary Sue Helm, Election Administrator
Suite 148, State Capitol
700 Capital Avenue
Frankfort, KY 40601-3493

Subject: Request for Petition Signature Waiver

Dear Ms. Helm:

Thank you and your staff for assistance and information received
to date.

Ms. Helm, I realize I do not have the good ol' boy Kentucky
political experience one acquires from being elected to a
prestigious state office, growing up in a politically oriented family
and, of course, from a wealthy Kentuckian dynasty that contributes
to politicians coffers. I'm just an American, repeat, American that
wants his country back.

I'm not saying Attorney General Jack Conway or Doctor Rand
Paul are not Americans by birth. What I am saying is they are
individuals of privilege. They have no knowledge the hardships

deployed military person and their families are subjected.

Yes, composition of the U.S. Military is of volunteers as the draft ended. However, they are not mercenaries hired to assure oil contracts in Kosovo and Iraq, provide security for the construction of oil pipelines through Helmand Province in Afghanistan or contribute to the death and destruction of the indigenous of Palestine.

When I joined the U.S. Air Force in 1960, just as the new enlistees do today, I stood near an American Flag and swore that I would defend the U.S. Constitution against all enemies both foreign and domestic. We also acknowledged we were to follow the orders of the President of the United States and the officers appointed over us. However, the Uniform Code of Military Justice, UCMJ, provides the military member with the ability to disobey orders he or she believes to be unlawful orders.

Naturally, if the member has the integrity to disobey an order, he or she under goes a sometime lengthy period of abuse and ridicule before a military jury and judge sets them free if the order was in fact unlawful. If lawful, the member will most probably go to a federal military prison.

To avoid such an incident, a member of Congress, should not have approved military action by the Presidential Administration. If the incident or situation warranted troops going into battle, then both houses of Congress should have declared a state of war. There have been no legal reason for a Declaration of War since the armed forces of the country of Japan bombed Pearl Harbor on December 7, 1941.

Moreover, it is doubtful the Attorney General Conway or Doctor Rand have ever lived and worked with the indigenous of Laos,

Thailand, and Saudi Arabia plus visited a number of Muslim countries. So what someone may say, I watch the news and read. The truth of an indigenous people, their religion, and their government requires being there.

I realize each state has rules which supplement Constitutional guidelines for national offices such as the President, Senate and the U.S. House of Representatives and as such have the authority to create hardships for those Americans willing to serve this great nation as an American. However, by doing so, the state prohibits a non-Democrat or non-Republican from presenting his or her grievances to the people as an Independent candidate.

Outstanding examples of a primary election's results which surprised Democrat and Republican leaders were in South Carolina and, of course, our state with the honorable Secretary of State, Mr. Trey Grayson. Most everyone, including myself, believed Secretary Grayson would win the Republican Primary. The South Carolina contest was won by a former U.S. Air Force and U.S. Army member, Mr. Alvin Greene, recently discharged from the armed forces.

One could think the logical ticket for Dr. Rand Paul would have been the Libertarian Party as he, in my opinion, did not conform to the Republican Party Platform. However, due to his father's influence, Congress Ron Paul, web sites were already in place for Dr. Rand Paul to solicit funds as a Republican Candidate.

Mr. Alvin Greene's efforts, which paid off, reminded me of a movie the Distinguished Gentlemen, starring Mr. Eddie Murphy. The setting was in South Florida where a Florida U.S. House of Representatives member had expired and Mr. Murphy campaigned as the deceased. You'd have to watch the movie.

Returning to the subject. I do not understand the large number of petition signatures required to place my name on the November ballot. I have been voted for twice during my attempts to unseat the honorable Harold Rogers of Kentucky's 5th U.S. Congressional District. In fact, I received respectable numbers of votes both in 2002 and 2004. (No one can unseat Congressman Rogers as he is among the leading earmark politicians for pork for their districts.) Too me, said voting, indicate the people would vote for me.

And, as during my 2002 and 2004 political attempts I do not accept donations. I will not spend more than the $5,000.00 allowed for a campaign without the U.S. Senate's Clerk oversight. As a disabled military veteran, my mobility is limited. I will have to hire a company or group to collect petition signatures which will create a needless hardship. I have been tested. (I recall a disabled Vietnam War veteran, the honorable Max Cleland, a triple amputee being elected U.S. Senator from the state of Georgia.)

Upsetting for me is that without the 5,000 petition signatures, Kentuckians have no knowledge of my candidacy. No major Kentucky newspaper will interview me or inform the public as I do not believe the state of Israel's economic and physical security supersedes the dictates of the U.S. Constitution. The United States is a republic, not a theocracy. I am an American

Ms. Helm is there any way I may receive a waiver for the required petition signatures?

I thank you for your attention and, hopefully, a favorable response.

With respect,

Billy Ray Wilson

209 Autumn Drive
London, KY 40744-7071
(606) 862-2847 phone
(606) 330-0124 fax
brwilson04@windstream.net

April 19, 2011

The Honorable Elaine Walker
Office of the Secretary of State
The Capitol Building
700 Capital Avenue
Suite 152
Frankfort, KY 40601

Subject: Denial of Due Process (2020 Senate Election)

Dear Madam Secretary:

Congratulations on your appointment to one of Kentucky's most important government position.

Secretary Walker with the 2012 National Elections fast approaching, it is my opinion that Kentucky's Election Policy must be reviewed to afford all Americans with an equal opportunity to express their grievances through the ballot box. In this light, I have provided background information regarding the subject.

Madam Secretary, you may not have learned of my campaign for the U.S. Senate, in 2010 as an Independent Candidate, due to the bias of our nations, especially Kentucky's, News Media. I am an American that paid his dues and stayed within the federal spending limit for said campaign; however, I was not afforded due process in my quest for the United States Senate.

Please before, I go an farther, I want to express my respect for the ladies that work in the Secretary's Election Division. The individuals were truly professional in their duties. Thank you.

When I speak of due process, I am addressing the voting ballots used by the counties for the 2010 Senate Election. To this end, I attach copies of election results retrieved from Kentucky's County Election Request for the identified year. You will note the breakdown of counties that identified, by name, my candidacy for the U.S. Senate while others on identified me as a "Write In."

Without a doubt, in my opinion, I was not afforded equal representation at the voting centers. I did not nor do not expect, the County Clerk or the clerks at the voting centers to campaign for me or any other candidate. However, I did expect, my name to be on the ballot and, if asked, the voter would be told the name of the Write In candidate. To my knowledge, there were those voting centers who did not know the names of the Write In candidates. (I was not the lone Independent Candidate.)

Regarding, name on the ballot, the Laurel County Clerk and I had heated words regarding my name on the ballot following a printed review of the November Ballot in the Sentinel-Echo Newspaper.

Moreover, the County Clerk said he was not going to campaign for me. I responded, I did not seek his assistance in campaigning only to identify me as the candidate either on the ballot or at the voting center. He declined.

And, if I am not mistaken, one of the ladies in your election office informed me that state policy was for the candidate to be identified. I mentioned this to the County Clerk and he remained belligerent.

As a native of Kentucky, I am not naïve to the dishonesty in Kentucky's political system with regards to Independent Candidates and Atheist. In this light, I've seen little change in the way our state conducts elections from when I was a young adult and today. Changes need to be made.

From the attachments, you will learn, in areas of higher learning and less emphasis on religion I did fairly well not have offered audio and visual campaign advertisement to our fellow Kentuckians. The cited failures and my lack of full mobility, plus of course, money restricted me from campaigning like my fellow candidates. I am an American, not a corporate prostitute.

Regarding religion. I published two books (My Struggle Too & Enough Is Enough) identifying my belief that religion is not a nationality and the United States is a Constitutional Republic, not a theocracy. (Naturally, the books were not well received within the Judeo-Christian areas of the state.) Also, I emphasized in 2002 Republican Primary that Iraq had no Weapons of Mass

Destruction, eliminating the welfare in U.S. Congressional District 5, and terminate all support and aid to the illegal country of Israel.) Of course there were other subjects of difference between the Congressman Harold Rogers but he would not debate me at a KET Political Campaign venue. The Congressman was a no show.

Madam Secretary, I have strayed from the subject. Forgive me.

I do not expect a change in the 2010 Senator Race but I would like to see Independent Candidates afforded equal recognition with the state's election process and, of course, the state's news media.

Again, congratulations of your posting and, hopefully, reorganization of Kentucky's Election System.

With respect, I remain.

BILLY RAY WILSON
American

Copy To: the Honorable Lisa Murkowski
             United States Senator
             709 Hart Senate Building
             Washington, DC 20510

ELAINE N. WALKER
SECRETARY OF STATE

COMMONWEALTH OF KENTUCKY
OFFICE OF THE SECRETARY OF STATE

SUITE 152, STATE CAPITOL
700 CAPITAL AVENUE
FRANKFORT, KY 40601-3493
(502) 564-3490
FAX (502) 564-5687
WEBSITE: WWW.SOS.KY.GOV

May 2, 2011

Mr. Billy Ray Wilson
209 Autumn Drive
London, KY 40744-7071

Dear Mr. Wilson:

This will acknowledge receipt of your correspondence regarding the casting and counting of write-in votes in the 2010 election for the Office of U.S. Senate.

Procedures relating to write-in candidates and the tabulating of write-in votes cast by voters are governed by KRS 117.265 (copy attached). County Clerks are required to provide to precinct election officers a certified list of persons who have filed declaration of intent to be a write-in candidate. At election training workshops conducted by the State Board of Elections county clerks have been advised that while there is a requirement to provide a certified list of write-in candidates to the precinct election officers, this list should not be posted in the precinct as there could be a violation of the electioneering statute. The certified list is provided only upon the request of a voter. (A copy of the applicable pages of training materials prepared by the State Board of Election's legal counsel relating to write-in candidates and write-in votes is enclosed.)

It appears that in those counties listing the write-in language only and not your name are those counties in which you did not receive a vote. Voters may have cast a write-in vote for other persons but only the write-in votes for persons who have filed a declaration of intent to be a write-in candidate are the only write-in votes that may be counted. We have enclosed a copy of the official vote totals for every county for each of the U.S. Senate candidates in the 2010 general election as certified to the Secretary of State by each county board of elections.

Any change in the counting or casting of a vote for a write-in candidate would require legislative action.

Thank you for your kind remarks regarding my appointment to the Office of Secretary of State and the compliments expressed in your correspondence to the staff in the Election Division and if we may further assist, please contact our office.

Sincerely,

Elaine N. Walker
Secretary of State

Enclosures (3)

Copy to: The Honorable Dean Johnson
Laurel County Clerk

117.265 Write-in votes.

(1) A voter may, at any regular or special election, cast a write-in vote for any person qualified as provided in subsection (2) or (3) of this section, whose name does not appear upon the ballot label for any office, by writing the name of his or her choice upon the appropriate device for the office being voted on provided on the voting machine as required by KRS 117.125. Any candidate for city office who is defeated in a partisan or nonpartisan primary shall be ineligible as a candidate for the same office in the regular election. Any voter utilizing an absentee ballot for a regular or special election may write in a vote for any eligible person whose name does not appear upon the ballot, by writing the name of his or her choice under the office.

(2) Write-in votes shall be counted only for candidates for election to office who have filed a declaration of intent to be a write-in candidate with the Secretary of State or county clerk, depending on the office being sought, on or before the fourth Friday in October preceding the date of the regular election and not later than the second Friday before the date of a special election. The declaration of intent shall be filed no earlier than the first Wednesday after the first Monday in November of the year preceding the year the office will appear on the ballot, and no later than 4 p.m. local time at the place of filing when filed on the last date on which papers may be filed. The declaration of intent shall be on a form prescribed by the Secretary of State.

(3) A person shall not be eligible as a write-in candidate:

(a) For more than one (1) office in a regular or special election; or

(b) If his or her name appears upon the ballot label for any office, except that the candidate may file a notice of withdrawal prior to filing an intent to be a write-in candidate for office when a vacancy in a different office occurs because of:

1. Death;

2. Disqualification to hold the office sought;

3. Severe disabling condition which arose after the nomination; or

4. The nomination of an unopposed candidate.

(4) Persons who wish to run for President and Vice-President shall file a declaration of intent to be a write-in candidate, along with a list of presidential electors pledged to those candidates, with the Secretary of State on or before the fourth Friday in October preceding the date of the regular election for those offices. The declaration of intent shall be filed no earlier than the first Wednesday after the first Monday in November of the year preceding the year the office will appear on the ballot, and no later than 4 p.m. local time at the place of filing when filed on the last date on which papers may be filed. Write-in votes cast for the candidates whose names appear on the ballot shall apply to the slate of pledged presidential electors, whose names shall not appear on the ballot.

(5) The county clerk shall provide to the precinct election officers certified lists of those persons who have filed declarations of intent as provided in subsections (2) and (3) of this section. Only write-in votes cast for qualified candidates shall be counted.

(6) Two (2) election officers of opposing parties shall upon the request of any voter instruct the voter on how to cast a write-in vote.

Effective: July 15, 2010

History: Amended 2010 Ky. Acts ch. 176, sec. 7, effective July 15, 2010. -- Amended 2008 Ky. Acts ch. 79, sec. 4, effective July 15, 2008. -- Amended 2005 Ky. Acts ch. 71, sec. 4, effective June 20, 2005. -- Amended 2002 Ky. Acts ch. 34, sec. 1, effective July 15, 2002. -- Amended 1998 Ky. Acts ch. 243, sec. 12, effective April 1, 1998. -- Amended 1992 Ky. Acts ch. 288, sec. 57, effective July 14, 1992; and ch. 454, sec. 1, effective July 14, 1992.. -- Amended 1990 Ky. Acts ch. 48, sec. 29, effective July 13, 1990; and ch. 366, sec. 2, effective July 13, 1990. -- Amended 1986 Ky. Acts ch. 287, sec. 10, effective July 15, 1986. -- Amended 1982 Ky. Acts ch. 394, sec. 16, effective July 15, 1982. -- Amended 1976 Ky. Acts ch. 247, sec. 6, effective June 19, 1976. -- Created 1974 Ky. Acts ch. 130, sec. 40, effective June 21, 1974.

Legislative Research Commission Note (7/14/92). This section was amended by 1992 Acts chs. 288 and 454 which are in conflict. Pursuant to KRS 446.250, Acts ch. 288 which was last enacted by the General Assembly prevails.

STATE BOARD OF ELECTIONS

ELECTION TRAINING SESSION

OCTOBER 15, 2008

TREY GRAYSON
SECRETARY OF STATE
CHAIRMAN

SARAH BALL JOHNSON
EXECUTIVE DIRECTOR

SANDY MILBURN
ASSISTANT DIRECTOR

STATE BOARD OF ELECTIONS MEMBERS

ROBERT GABLE
BILL KIRKLAND
GREG SHUMATE

GEORGE RUSSELL
DENISE MAY
ROY SIZEMORE

WRITE-*INS & OUTS*

Common Questions About Write-Ins:

Q. When can write-in votes be cast?

A. At any regular or special election, a voter may cast a write-in vote on a voting machine or an absentee ballot for any person qualified whose name does not appear upon the ballot label as a candidate. KRS 117.265(1).

Q. What if the voter has failed to fill in the box, arrow, or oval on a paper ballot, but has written in the name of an eligible write-in candidate? Do we count the vote?

A. **No.** 31 KAR 6:030, Uniform Definition of a Vote, requires that the voter fill in both the box, arrow or oval on the paper ballot, as well as write-in the name of an eligible write-in candidate. **See Section 4(3)(A) and Section 5(2)(a).**

Q. Who is a Qualified Write-In Candidate?

A. A qualified write-in candidate for election to office who has filed a declaration of intent to be a write-in candidate, SBE/SOS/01, SBE/SOS/02, SBE/SOS/03, with the Secretary of State or county clerk, depending on the office being sought. KRS 117.265(2).

Q. When I publish the ballot as required by KRS Chapter 424 am I required to publish the list of qualified write-in candidates?

A. **No.** KRS 424.290 only requires the publishing of a copy of "the pertinent information that will appear upon which the voters will cast their votes at a particular polling place." The Attorney General has determined this to mean only a summary of the ballot as it will appear on the voting machine. OAG 67-203 and OAG 66-295. Since Write-in candidates do not appear on the voting machine ballot face, then you do not have to publish the list in the newspaper.

Q. Should I instruct the precinct officers to post the list of write-in candidates at the precinct?

A. **No.** The county clerk shall provide to the precinct election officers certified lists of those persons who have filed declarations of intent to be write-in candidates. KRS 117.265(5). However, you need to train your precinct officers that they **must not post** this list at the precinct because they could be violating the electioneering prohibition. KRS 117.235(3). This list **should only** be provided to the public upon request and should not be volunteered.

Q.   **Should I include the list of write-in candidates when sending absentee ballots?**

A.   **No.** The list of write-in candidates mentioned in KRS 117.265(5) *should only* be provided to the public upon request and should not be volunteered. Otherwise, you could be violating the electioneering prohibition. KRS 117.235(3).

Q.   **Can a write-in candidate request and witness a recanvass?**

A.   **Yes.**   The Attorney General has determined that a write-in candidate is a candidate within the meaning of KRS 117.305 where he is, in fact, an active candidate, and would qualify to request the county election commission to recheck the voting machines. 1958 OAG 42,433.

KRS § 117.305 (1) ". . .a *candidate* makes a written request to the county board of elections in the case of a candidate who has filed with the county clerk, or the Secretary of State in the case of a candidate who has filed with the Secretary of State, to check and recanvass the voting machines and absentee ballots of any precinct or any number of precincts involving his race. . .At the recanvass, each political party represented on the board may appoint a representative there to be its governing body, and also *each candidate* to be voted for may be present, either in person or by a representative or both."

Q.   **Can write-in candidates designate their own challengers?**

A.   **No.** The Attorney General has determined that "this statute authorizes the various political parties who have nominated candidates in the primary *whose names are on the ballot* in November to select challengers. At the same time school board candidates and independent candidates who have filed and *whose names are on the ballot* are entitled to designate a challenger for each precinct." OAG 77-654.

KRS § 117.315 (3) "the county executive committee of any political party having a ticket to elect at any regular election may designate not more than two (2) challengers to be present at and witness the holding of the election in each precinct in the county."

KRS § 117.315 (2) "any school board candidate, any independent ticket or candidate for city office, any nonpartisan city candidate, or candidate for an office of the Court of Justice at the primary or regular election may designate not more than one (1) challenger to be present at and witness the holding of primaries or elections in each precinct in the county."

Q.   **Can write-in candidates witness the vote count?**

A.   **Yes and No.** Write-in candidates can witness the counting of the absentee ballots in the clerk's office, but there is no mention in Kentucky law that allows write-in candidates to witness the tally of the machines at the precinct or the tally of the precincts at the clerk's office.

Pursuant to KRS 117.087 (3) "candidates or their representatives shall be permitted to be present" for the counting of the absentee ballots in the county clerk's office. This appears to mean **any** candidate, including write-in candidates.

KRS 117.275 does not address whether the county board of elections can allow representatives to witness the vote count at the precinct or in the clerk's office on behalf of write-in candidates.

KRS 117.275(7) "in regular elections, the governing authority of each political party, each candidate for member of board of education, independent candidate, or independent ticket may designate a representative to the county board of elections to witness and check the vote count. The county board of elections shall authorize representatives of the news media to observe the taking of the tally of votes from the voting machine in each precinct in each primary, regular or special election."

KRS 117.275(1) "at the count of the votes *in any precinct*, any candidate or slate of candidates and any representatives to witness and check the count of the votes therein, who are authorized to be appointed as is provided in subsection (7) of this section. Shall be admitted and be permitted to be present and witness the count."

BILLY RAY WILSON

Master Sergeant, USAF (Retired)

209 Autumn Drive
London, KY 40744-7071
(606) 862-2847 phone
(606) 330-0124 fax
brwilson04@windstream.net e-mail

May 3, 2011

The Honorable Elaine Walker
Kentucky's Secretary of State
700 Capital Avenue
Suite 152, State Capitol
Frankfort, KY 40601-3493

Dear Madam Secretary:

This letter acknowledges your letter of May 2, 2011 regarding
the 2010 Senatorial Election Results, with remarks, and
present my views on our countries political uncertainty.

Madam Secretary before I proceed, I would like to inform you I
will not be burdening your office with any future plans to run
for elective office. My physical will not allow such an
endeavor and I should not have sought public office in 2010.
(I had to have a lady driver and assistant at times.)

I read your voting numbers very carefully and compared then
with Kentucky's Web Site results for the 2010 Senatorial
Election. There is a discrepancy: Web Site read 1,214 for
me. Your totals are 338. (Just a point of interest.)

of Drug Enforcement should allow the farmers and manufacturers of Kentucky to grow and produce products from a centuries old plant - HEMP. However, in my opinion, when I addressed cutting back on Washington Pork in the 5th District, I caught the attention of the welfare community and the dishonest politicians of the region..

For my Senate race, I ran on the same topics but addressed the need for our Department of Justice to indicate and, if found guilty, impose the death penalty of former President George W. Bush and Vice President Richard Cheney.

No Bush and Cheney did not write or approve the 1998 Iraq Liberation Act which charged President Clinton with removing Saddam Hussein as Iraq's Head of States. (President Clinton, as you know, did not order the invasion of Afghanistan or Iraq.)

Moreover, President Clinton did not take seriously the warning from Osama bin Laden, leader of Al-Qaeda, that his organization would attack the U.S. and her resources in compliance with his (bin Laden's) Declaration of War against the United States.

Enter President Bush and Vice President Cheney's Religious Crusade against Muslims. (A number of news agencies reported President Bush stated that God told him to remove Saddam Hussein.) From Afghanistan to Iraq, the Bush Administration killed our military personnel, robbed the national treasury and destroyed international relations with the members of the United Nations.

President Obama came to office without a majority from the state of Kentucky. The why is because of racism, lack of education and engrained religious teachings passed down from generation to generation. A change must take place.

And, Democrats and Republicans in the Commonwealth and most Red States are like sporting events between opposing teams. Their minds, body and spirit are for their teams, not the Commonwealth or the nation. To this end, our nation, especially Kentucky, reminds one of the Holy Roman Empire. History does repeat herself.

Ms. Walker, I am not bitter. I want my country back to vision of our founders and this fact will never be achieved unless Independent Candidates are afforded the same opportunity as Democrats and Republicans.

Kentucky

My fellow Kentuckians, as an American and native of the Commonwealth, I want our government returned to the people. To accomplish this awesome task, I seek the Office of the United States Senate as an Independent Candidate.

As a candidate from a non-established political party, I must obtain 5,000 petition signatures from registered voters. The signatures, along with $500.00, would place my name on the November 2010 ballot. (Please, no monetary donations.) Petitions and money must be delivered to the Secretary of States' Office no later than August 10, 2010.

Should you allow me my Constitutional Right to seek said political office, please sign the afforded Kentucky Form SBE 59-2. After signing, please fold the Announcement of Candidacy Form letter in a manner, plus add postage, that will allow return mailing.

With respect,

Billy Ray Wilson

Billy Ray Wilson

BILLY RAY WILSON
209 AUTUMN DRIVE
LONDON, KY 40744-7071

INBOX > EMAIL MESSAGE

Folders [manage]   ◇ Prev | Next ◇

Inbox (1)   Move to: Drafts

Sent Mail

Trash (7)

Date: Monday, October 4, 2010 6:19 PM
From: Donald N. Sims <dnsims@gmail.com>
To: brwilson04@windstream.net
Subject: Updates
Size: 761 KB
Attachments: Bill Wilson (US Senate 1).jpg (467.4 KB)

Mailbox Usage

You are using 1% of
your mailbox (7 MB
out of 1,000 MB)

Bill Wilson (US Senate 2).jpg (289.2 KB)

Mr. Wilson,

Here are the updates you asked for and I have made the changes to the audio but it will probably be tomorrow before my production man can cut it. But, here are the 2 slide for you to view.

Let me know if there is anything else I can help you with.

Thanks,
Donald Sims

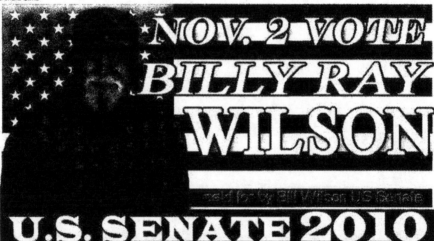

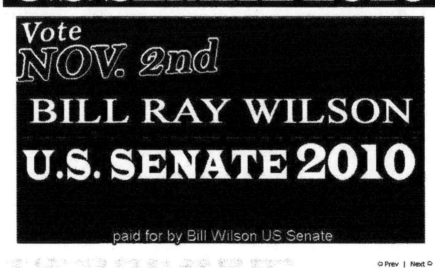

◇ Prev | Next ◇

2010 General Election

Website last updated 11/24/2010 11:41:26 AM EST

Registered Voters:	2,885,775	
Ballots Cast:	1,411,695	
Voter Turnout:	48.92 %	

Counties Partially Reported:	0 of 120
Counties Completely Reported:	120 of 120
Counties Percent Reported:	100.00 %

OFFICIAL RESULTS

Precinct level results by county and race are located under the "Results by County" tab above.

(263 of 263)

Go To Page 1   Display 5

US Senator

120 of 120 Counties Reporting

	Percent	Votes
Rand PAUL (REP)	55.69%	755,411
Jack CONWAY (DEM)	44.22%	599,843
WRITE-IN	0.09%	1,214
		1,356,468

US Representative, 1st Congressional District

34 of 34 Counties Reporting

	Percent	Votes
Edward WHITFIELD (REP)	71.25%	153,519
Charles Kendall HATCHETT (DEM)	28.75%	61,960
		215,479

US Representative, 2nd Congressional District

21 of 21 Counties Reporting

	Percent	Votes
S. Brett GUTHRIE (REP)	67.89%	155,906
Ed MARKSBERRY (DEM)	32.11%	73,749
		229,655

US Representative, 3rd Congressional District

1 of 1 Counties Reporting

		Percent	Votes
Todd LALLY (REP)		44.01%	112,627
John YARMUTH (DEM)		54.68%	139,940
Michael D. HANSEN		0.52%	1,334
Edward A. MARTIN (LIB)		0.79%	2,029
			255,930

US Representative, 4th Congressional District

24 of 24 Counties Reporting

		Percent	Votes
Geoff DAVIS (REP)		69.48%	151,774
John WALTZ (DEM)		30.52%	66,675
			218,449

Powered by -

Commonwealth of Kentucky
Trey Grayson, Secretary of State

November 2, 2010
Official 2010 General Election Results

For the office of
US Senator

US Senator

	Republican Party Rand Paul	Democratic Party Jack Conway	Write-in Billy Ray Wilson
Adair	4,498	2,032	0
Allen	4,277	2,115	2
Anderson	4,572	3,523	4
Ballard	1,647	1,362	0
Barren	7,458	5,385	0
Bath	1,409	1,981	0
Bell	5,269	3,236	0
Boone	24,331	8,363	2
Bourbon	3,026	2,818	1
Boyd	7,067	7,173	0
Boyle	4,960	3,880	1
Bracken	1,765	1,392	0
Breathitt	2,023	2,464	0
Breckinridge	3,686	2,757	0
Bullitt	14,547	8,608	0
Butler	2,699	1,283	0
Caldwell	2,544	2,114	0
Calloway	6,134	4,386	1
Campbell	18,386	9,948	0
Carlisle	1,249	969	0
Carroll	1,509	1,807	0
Carter	3,797	4,475	0
Casey	3,207	1,135	0
Christian	8,832	5,410	2
Clark	6,287	4,485	0
Clay	3,712	1,270	0
Clinton	2,844	884	0

Trey Grayson, Secretary of State

2010 General Election Results

	Republican Party	Democratic Party	Write-In
	Rand Paul	Jack Conway	Billy Ray Wilson
Crittenden	2,053	1,316	6
Cumberland	1,978	686	0
Daviess	16,930	13,858	0
Edmonson	2,656	1,730	1
Elliott	493	991	0
Estill	2,607	1,901	0
Fayette	43,313	44,591	17
Fleming	2,445	2,627	0
Floyd	4,794	6,360	0
Franklin	7,912	10,654	13
Fulton	1,045	1,009	0
Gallatin	1,619	1,167	0
Garrard	3,617	1,693	0
Grant	3,882	2,147	0
Graves	7,087	5,346	0
Grayson	5,443	3,133	10
Green	2,926	1,622	2
Greenup	5,862	5,750	4
Hancock	1,444	1,719	0
Hardin	16,064	11,271	8
Harlan	4,934	3,455	0
Harrison	3,035	2,596	4
Hart	2,748	2,268	1
Henderson	6,650	6,885	6
Henry	2,992	2,551	3
Hickman	947	733	0
Hopkins	9,051	6,274	2
Jackson	3,421	1,015	0
Jefferson	114,435	143,385	1
Jessamine	10,197	5,468	2
Johnson	5,216	2,692	0

	Republican Party	Democratic Party	Write-In
	Rand Paul	Jack Conway	Billy Ray Wilson
Kenton	29,372	14,582	2
Knott	2,720	3,067	0
Knox	5,664	3,267	3
Larue	2,729	1,865	0
Laurel	11,472	3,927	2
Lawrence	2,685	2,207	0
Lee	1,639	1,040	0
Leslie	3,530	916	0
Letcher	3,856	3,540	0
Lewis	2,436	1,080	0
Lincoln	4,072	3,169	0
Livingston	2,090	1,792	4
Logan	5,061	3,087	4
Lyon	1,727	1,475	3
Madison	13,737	10,401	117
Magoffin	2,504	3,143	0
Marion	2,349	3,029	15
Marshall	6,689	5,254	5
Martin	2,453	1,226	0
Mason	2,724	2,282	1
McCracken	13,629	8,601	12
McCreary	3,417	1,375	0
McLean	1,731	1,826	4
Meade	4,984	4,269	1
Menifee	869	1,520	0
Mercer	4,501	3,125	8
Metcalfe	2,112	1,783	1
Monroe	3,488	1,098	0
Montgomery	3,864	3,986	0
Morgan	1,733	2,334	0
Muhlenberg	4,019	4,945	0

Trey Grayson, Secretary of State

2010 General Election Results

County	Republican Party Rand Paul	Democratic Party Jack Conway	Write-In Billy Ray Wilson
Nelson	7,706	6,502	0
Nicholas	882	1,087	0
Ohio	4,498	4,021	1
Oldham	14,932	7,248	8
Owen	1,968	1,458	0
Owsley	1,199	634	0
Pendleton	2,525	1,472	0
Perry	4,834	3,833	0
Pike	7,663	7,470	1
Powell	1,758	2,116	0
Pulaski	14,209	5,001	11
Robertson	373	373	0
Rockcastle	3,182	1,301	0
Rowan	2,883	3,752	0
Russell	4,443	1,786	1
Scott	8,577	6,250	1
Shelby	8,734	5,609	1
Simpson	2,846	2,065	0
Spencer	4,295	2,562	0
Taylor	5,539	3,977	16
Todd	2,283	1,545	0
Trigg	3,301	2,254	0
Trimble	1,432	1,291	0
Union	2,513	2,516	0
Warren	18,651	11,686	1
Washington	2,480	1,904	1
Wayne	3,868	2,835	0
Webster	2,195	1,909	1
Whitley	6,469	2,594	1
Wolfe	737	1,122	0
Woodford	5,344	4,520	19

Commonwealth of Kentucky   Trey Grayson, Secretary of State   2010 General Election Results

	Republican Party	Democratic Party	Write-In
	Rand Paul	Jack Conway	Billy Ray Wilson
Total Votes	755,706	600,052	338

SENATE EXPENDITURES

DATE	PURPOSE	COST
10 March 2010	WEB SITE	$500.00
15 March 2010	Volunteer advertisement	$ 63.20
16 March 2010	Yard Sign	$ 21.20
18 March 2010	Yard Sign	$ 85.00
19 March 2010	Office Supplies	$ 14.50
23 March 2010	Postage Stamps	$ 44.00
26 March 2010	Printer Ink.	$ 44.95
30 March 2010	Paper, cards, illumination	$ 26.72
10 April 2010	Petition Signature Purpose	$ 16.89
24 April 2010	Web fee (monthly)	$ 24.99
18 May 2010	Web fee (monthly)	$ 24.99
18 May 2010	Changes to website	$ 32.50
27 May 2010	Postal Mailings	$ 16.80
28 May 2010	Postal Mailings	$ 2.10
30 June 2010	Web fee (monthly)	$ 24.99
02 July 2010	Political Flyer (11,633 copies)	$460.56
24 July 2010	Web fee (monthly)	$ 24.99
25 July 2010	Write In Candidate Fee	$ 50.00
31 July 2010	Photo - Political	$ 8.47
31 July 2010	Mailing photo SOS	$ .88

02 Aug. 2010	Campaign cards (500)	$ 52.00
04 Aug 2010	Revise Web Site	$ 32.50
20 Aug 2010	Web fee (monthly)	$ 24.99
10 Sep 2010	Candidate Photos	$ 29.00
17 Sep 2010	Hotel (Ashland)	$349.41
17 Sep 2010	Gasoline	$ 36.00
21 Sep 2010	visual aids	$ 29.60
23 Sep 2010	Booth for Forum	$ 50.00
24 Sep 2010	Talking Paper 100 copies	$ 59.36
24 Sep 2010	Photo Flyers 100 copies	$ 10.60
25 Sep 2010	Gas $2.67x7 gal (Frankfort)	$ 12.69
29 Sep 2010	Web Fee (monthly)	$ 24.99
30 Sep 2010	Holiday Inn (Campbellsville)	$ 77.13
30 Sep 2010	Gas $2.51X6.4 (Campbellsville)	$ 16.64
04 Oct 2010	Office Depot (Cards/e-mail photo)	$ 40.00
05 Oct 2010	On-Screen Political Ad	$275.00
06 Oct 2010	E-Mail photo to newspaper	$ 1.32
07 Oct 2010	E-Mail photo to newspaper	$ 2.92
11 Oct 2010	Political Add (Sentinel-Echo)	$170.00
12 Oct 2010	Newspaper advertisement	$999.00
12 Oct 2010	Holiday Inn Express (Eminence)	$85.00
12 Oct 2010	Fuel 9.4X $2.68 (Eminence)	$25.19
13 Oct 2010	Copies Made 200	$19.95

13 Oct 2010	Posters made	$63.15
15 Oct 2010	E-Mail Photo (SOS KY)	$ 3.74
22 Oct 2010	Web Site Update	$32.50
15 Oct 2010	Web fee	$24.99
19 Oct 2010	French Inn (Maysville)	$153.83
19/20 Oct 2010	Fuel 13.5 X $2.75 (Maysville & Lebanon, KY)	$37.12
19/20 Oct 2010	Driver	$150.00
24 Oct 2010	Copies of Talking Paper	$42.40
25 Oct 2010	Horseshoe Hotel	$77.69
25-26 Oct 2010	Fuel 11.3 X $2.75	$31.01
Total Cost of Political Campaign		$4,357.45

Biography

Over the past months, I have read a number of biographies of leading political candidates and incumbents such Senator Jim Bunning and Senator Mitch McConnell. As one would suspect, I have nothing in common with them or, for example, Secretary Trey Grayson or Doctor Rand Paul. I am an American from Kentucky that wants the U.S. Constitution returned as the foundation for the government of the United States of America.

My life began on September 21, 1943 at the home of my father's half sister in East Bernstadt, KY. My father was in the United States Marine Corps and my mother was a housewife, the best mother one could have, and she worked part-time to support our family. (My parents divorced the last time in 1955.) I have an older and younger sister.

A few years following the divorce of my parents, nine days after my 17th birthday, I joined the United States Air Force. (My mother had to sign and approve my enlistment.) My mother re-married. Needless to write, the step father and I did not see eye to eye.

I've been married and divorced twice. One daughter, May 7, 1965, by my first wife and a son (August 17, 1970), out-of-wedlock, while assigned in the Kingdom of Laos. At my return to the United States following my Laotian tour, I brought my son with me. His mother, a Thai woman, did not want to leave Southeast Asia. I paid an aunt in Detroit, Michigan to raise my son. No children with the second wife.

During my career in the United States Air Force, I was fortunate or unfortunate, depending on one's point of view, to have been assigned to sensitive assignments at the U.S. Embassy, Vientiane, Kingdom of Laos and the Joint Casualty Resolution Center (JCRC) Nakhon Phanom Royal Thai Air Base, Kingdom of Thailand. These assignments required a Top Secret Clearance.

The Laotian assignment was as a Mister and without military status. At the Air Attache Defense Mission,, we ran the United States' illegal air war in Laos. The JCRC assignment was more stressful than the Laotian tour as our mission was to go into Cambodia, Laos and Vietnam and recover the remains of U.S. Missing In Action. When not in the field, assignees reviewed classified documents from numerous sources in an attempt to resolve MIA status. We, JCRC, changed MIA status' to Deceased, Body Not Recovered or Deceased, Body Not Recoverable.

A few months prior to my retirement from the United States Air Force, I learned the U.S. Air Force was going to hire military retirees to train Royal Saudi Air Force Warrant Officers in applicable air force specialties. To this end, over the following 6 non-consecutive years I was assigned to King Khaild Air Base, Asir Province, Kingdom of Saudi Arabia. We lived and worked side by side with all Saudi's from the enlisted, the senior command officers and members of the Saudi Royal Family.

And, I might add, what you read and hear from the national news media regarding the Kingdom of Saudi Arabia and the people of the Middle East are in most part lies. For example, since 1956, one may practice his or her own religion or not worship a religious entity. The only stipulation was the non-Muslim not attempt to disseminate religious literature or covert Muslims to another religion. Religion was to be practiced at our compounds.

In between employment assignments, in the Middle East, I was employed by London's Storm Security as a security consultant for one month in Nassau, Bahamas. Kentucky Supervisor for Pony Express Courier Service for less than 90 days. A housekeeping supervisor for 60 days at the Grand Teton Lodge, Wyoming. Travel Clerk and Testing Office at the Phoenix Military Entrance Processing Station, Phoenix, Arizona for a little over 2 1/1 years, My last employment was with the Department of Veterans Affairs Medical Centers at Allen Park, Michigan and Louisville, Kentucky. I was medically retired in 1998 from the Louisville Medical Center as an Administrative Officer of the Day.

During the 35 years of employment, I received a number of awards, ribbons, and medals for example: United States Air Force Meritorious Service Medal, Bronze Star with 1 Oak Leaf Cluster; Joint Service Commendation Medal; Army Outstanding Unit Award, Air Force Commendation Medal with 1 Silver Oak Leaf Cluster, Air Force Longevity Service Ribbon with 4 Oak Leaf Cluster; National Defense Service Medal; Vietnam Service Medal with 9 Bronze Stars; Air Force Outstanding Unit Award with 4 Combat "V" Devices. At the VA Medical Center, Allen Park, Michigan, one of my suggestions saved the U.S. Governments hundreds of thousands of dollars. (My share of the award allowed me to travel to Australia for two weeks.)

And, of course, one received monetary awards and certificates for outstanding work performance. Of interest was: Northrop Aircraft Service Division's (Air Force Contract) Trainer of the Quarter that came with a $1.000.00 bonus.

Earlier I identified the prestigious assignments of my career. It was at these assignments, I learned of the abuse of our Constitution and the lack of integrity by individuals in positions of power within the United States government and/or Departments of the government.

After my medical retirement in 1998, I returned back home to London in 2001. Within several months after returning, I unsuccessfully ran, as a Republican Candidate, against the Honorable Harold Rogers in 2002 and 2004. To this end, one can never unseat Congressman Rogers as he builds on the welfare and criminal base in Kentucky's 5th U.S. Congressional District. (What 2/3 of the 5th District receiving some type government subsistence.)

Moreover, I informed my fellow citizens throughout whatever mode available that there were no Weapons of Mass Destruction in Iraq and pointed out other lies by the Bush Administration. No one listened. Didn't want to loose their freebees.

Of note, to question my religious status, per the United States Constitution, is illegal but in tune with Kentucky's culture I submit: I am a deist.

And, although none were sold by national book stores, I am the author of two books: My Struggle Too, March 30, 2007, and Enough Is Enough, December 7, 2009. The publisher was Author House.

Recently, while in Corbin, I went in to "Books-A-Million" bookstore. I asked the attendant if they carried my book "Enough is Enough" in stock. She checked the computerized files. There was an annotation on the screen that identified my book saying the book was not for store display. However, should someone come in with a specific order for the book, the store would order and send the book to the buyer's home address.

The book "My Struggle Too" didn't have a chance. At a book signing in London, Jews and pro-Israel guests pointed at the name of the book and seated themselves. I suppose the reason was Adolph Hitler's published book ""My Struggle".

It is my opinion that no religion has the right of nationality. After all, religion is nothing but a belief. To this end, Jews in Germany were responsible for their own imprisonment and death camps.

I am an Independent candidate seeking, against medical advise, seeking the seat of retiring U.S. Senator Jim Bunning.

2010 Post Election Critique

Dear Americans of our beloved Commonwealth,

Sorry, for taking to so long to let you know our election results: 1,214 votes.

I want to thank each and everyone that voted for not just me but the Constitution of the United States of America.

My days of on the road politics are over but not my hopes for a better future for our nation. (My mind wants to keep going but the physical body is saying no.) However, let us find a General Dwight David Eisenhower that will step up and once again make our nation, the country envisioned by those brave colonists in 1776.

Speaking of on the road, I always believe the Commonwealth was the most beautiful and had the possibility of being the most influential state of the United States and my political travels confirmed that belief.

My goodness, the Commonwealth has waterways, outstanding highways, airports with 24/7 capability, farm areas for livestock to graze and family farmers to grow agriculture products to sustain the nation. Fossil fuel reserves but, equally important, the Commonwealth has the environment for the production of bio-fuels, wind turbine electricity, and on and on.

The only factor we need to succeed is the will of the young people to learn and adhere to the spirit and vision of the Declaration of Independence and the dictates of the United States Constitution. The founders of this nation never promised anything free to anyone. One must earn their way through life and/or be supported by a love one.

Moreover, the type of government turned over to the people by our founders was a Republic. This means we, the citizens, of the United States are the government. We do not need any outside force to build and keep our nation.

On a political note, I confirmed outside forces are active in the nation's political forum; therefore, the following lengthy narrative addresses foreign involvement in the affairs of the United States of America.

Subject: Unregistered Foreign Agents for the Socialist Country of Israel

An article in Thursday, November 4, 2010, Herald-Leader revealed, from post election poll canvassing, four out of five Kentuckians voted for Doctor Rand Paul because of the religious political ads ran by both Attorney General Jack Conway and Dr. Rand Paul.

Attorney General Conway questioned why Rand Paul, as a student, would join a fraternity outlawed by the school's administrator? Dr. Rand Paul's team finessed Conway's statements in to a negative message for Kentucky's religious zealots.

November 5, 2010 Herald-Leader Cartoonist, Joel Pett, continued the Aqua Buddha conversation, with a cartoon depicting Senator Mitch McConnell, Senator-Elect Rand Paul walking down a red carpet to pay homage to a large bag of the Almighty D'Allah. A statue of the Aqua Buddha was situated on the carpet.

In the same Herald-Leader publication, there was a similar text article written by Mr. Henry Olsen at the American Enterprise Institute, Washington, DC. The subject: Troubling trends: "GOP wins with whites, less educated." However, within the text, Mr. Olsen contends "Working-class whites voted Republican primarily because they intensely dislike President Barack Obama . The GOP captured about 10 percent of blacks' support and a third of Hispanics."

Yes! President Obama did very poorly in the Commonwealth, especially within Kentucky's 5th U.S. Congressional District, during the 2008 Presidential Election. (The votes he did receive came from the better educated and informed citizen.) The reason for the inherent prejudice, in my opinion, may be rooted from hand me down religious beliefs taught during the U.S. Civil War era.)

For the record, the United States of America is not a Judeo-Christian (Theocracy) Governed Nation. Our form of government is a Constitutional Republic. Individuals, in my opinion, that spread untruths should be charged with subversion and, equally important, have to register as a foreign agent for the Socialist Country of Israel.

Moreover, Article 6, paragraph 3, of the United States Constitution, informs Americans: no religious prerequisite mandatory to seek public office. (Actions by Attorney General Conway and Dr. Rand Paul were a slap at the generational religious beliefs of the people of Kentucky.)

Equally frustrating, in my opinion, too many Kentuckians participate in national and state elections as if the elections were a sporting event. For example, the Republican Party is the University of Kentucky Wildcats. The Democratic Party is the Louisville Cardinals. (Or vice-versa.)

And, there are Kentuckians who would vote for the political party's mascot. Existing difficulties, such as our country's engagement in to two illegal wars, allowing members of Congress to have dual citizenship and the Vice President of the United States acknowledgment he was a Zionist, didn't register. The party came first.

And, too many have forgotten the functions of the three branches of the U.S. Federal Government. For example, the President of the United States is the administrator of laws, regulations, policies that are designed to keep our nation safe, our people employed via creating a well regulated commerce and an expeditious flow of U.S. Mail.

The United States Congress, U.S. House of Representatives and U.S. Senate, is responsible for the oversight of the U.S. Presidential Administration to assure the dictates of the U.S. Constitution are adhered.

Should an enemy force physically attack the United States or our territories, it is the responsibility for the U.S. Congress to Declare an Act of War. (The President has the authority to deploy forces for a short period of time until such time Congress can convene to either approve funds for the war or deny funding. If funding is denied, then military forces will return to the barracks.) In no instance must the U.S. Congress, through legislative action, fund and force the U.S. President to remove a sovereign nation's Head of State. (Reference: 1998 Iraq Liberation Act.)

Nor, should U.S. Congressional lawmakers flood the White House and the media with letters and news releases complaining about the Obama administration's unprecedented scolding of Israeli Prime Minister Binyamin Netanyahu. (As usual, the Israeli Government approved the building of more illegal settlements on Palestinian land. President Obama wants to end the on-going, since May 1948, genocidal actions by the Hebrew Arabs (Jews) against their Palestinian Arab cousins. Zionist in our country do not want peace.)

Going further, Senator Sam Brownback, R-KS, not only berated the President because of the administration's support for a two state solution in Palestine but wants to move the U.S. Israeli Embassy to Jerusalem. (A clear violation of United Nations Resolutions.) Per the U.S. Constitution, the President of the United States is the administrator of U.S. Foreign Policy. Yes, Congress does have an oversight responsibility.

The Justices of the U.S. Supreme Court are charged per the U.S. Constitution to debate and deliver a majority vote on laws and/other actions set forth by the Presidential Administration and/or the U.S. Congress. (Too me allowing U.S. Corporations and other entities to flood the political area with unlimited and unaccounted funds are not Constitutional. So went the 2010 National Election.)

Of note, November 5, 2010, the national news media reported that Republican leader, the Honorable Mitch McConnell, declared President Obama must be a one term President. The GOP had too many policies President Obama was blocking. (I suspect two of the policies were the invasion of Iran and allowing the Israeli to proceed with the plans for a Greater Israel.) President John F. Kennedy and Attorney General Robert Kennedy attempted to rein in Israeli expansion but failed due to the murder of the President Kennedy and Attorney General Kennedy.

As an American retired (disabled) military veteran, I sought the Office of the United States Senate being vacated by the Honorable Jim Bunning (R-KY). I chose to seek the office as an Independent Candidate because my country is more than a sporting event or belief that an unproven religious entity is more important than the sovereignty of the United States of America.

Both the Democrat and Republican Parties have their own agendas for our country's resources. The agendas do not concern the American people but special interest groups and corporation wealth.

Following months of correspondence, visits to the Laurel County Clerk's Office, and related political activities, I was listed on the Commonwealth's U.S. Candidate List as a Write In candidate.

However, to my knowledge, no national news agency identified me as a qualified Senatorial Candidate nor following the election, post votes received.

Not understanding why at least one national news media did not identify my candidacy, I sent an e-mail to Diane Sawyer, ABC News, and Katie Couric, CBS News. I received a formatted e-mail response from ABC, No response from CBS

The failure of the national news media recognize my candidacy really floored me as they recognized the former unemployed Army/Air Force individual (Mr. Alvin Greene) from South Carolina. To Greene's credit he did win the Democratic Primary as a candidate for the U.S. Senate.

More frustrating was the report, Mr. Greene had only paid the large dollar amount to become a candidate for the U.S. Senate in South Carolina. Allegedly, he had no web site, campaign literature or other entities associated with a political campaign. (Mr. Greene is awaiting a court date in response to a felony charge.)

Regarding my campaign, I established a website; www.americanforussenate.com. Campaign business cards were purchased. A few yard signs were distributed, Talking Papers written and distributed identifying my platform. Two separate inserts were distributed throughout the state via the Lexington Herald-Leader Newspaper. I attended a number of political forums at key cities within the Commonwealth. I accepted no donations. For the London Community, I ran a political advertisement for one month at London's Regency Cinema.

My e-mail address, brwilson04@windstream.net, phone number, 606-862-2874, and fax number, (606) 330-0124 became personal and campaign numbers.

Reviewers of my website (13 comments) found my website well organized but my platform offended them. I was labeled a racist, an anti-Semite, crazy, and ignorant. One particular person accused me of using vulgar names for different ethnic groups.

Regarding the charge of racist: I am an American that adheres to the words of the Declaration of Independence and the U.S. Constitution. We are all Americans. There are no hyphenated Americans in the United States. We are all Americans.

The charge of anti-Semitism was not unusual. It is a known fact I regard the illegal nation of Israel as an affront to humanity. Hebrews Arabs (Jews) have been killing any and all that might obstruct Zionist goal of a greater Israel for centuries. To this end: 1. Judaism is a religion, not a nationality or citizenship legally in the international community except for the Socialist Country of Israel. 2. Personally, I do not care if your religious entity is your right big toe. Build a altar, put a picture of your toe on coffee mugs or whatever, I do not care. However, when religion dictate the political decisions of this nation, I take exception and will at the peril of death attempt to protect my country.

I may be crazy and ignorant but my love is for the United States of America. I have no loyalty except to the United States.

Now to vulgarism. I will be the first to acknowledge there was a time in my life that I did use a lot of profanity and some today. However, never in my life did I use vulgar names to identify an ethnic group. The words the reviewer used, I learned from watching movies.

Most Kentucky news media have been bias and/or non-attentive. To my knowledge only the Lebanon Enterprise identified me as opposing the Democrat and Republican candidates. The Sentinel-Echo, my hometown newspaper, provided each Senatorial Candidate with the same amount of column space and photograph to identify themselves and their platform.

Friday morning, November 5, 2010, the Sentinel-Echo Newspaper, London, KY, published the November 2, 2010, election results via precincts.. To my surprise, I received two votes: One from an Absentee Machine; the other from Absentee Mail. Regarding other votes, I can not say there were any; however, friends informed me they did vote for me. I know of one confirmed vote. I voted for myself. Where is that vote?

After reading the election print-out provided by the Sentinel-Echo, I contacted Kentucky's Secretary of State and Election Council. I was informed there were 10 counties not reporting; however, votes should be posted within a few days.

With the election over, I scanned the Internet to find any national media confirmation of my candidacy. To date, none exists. A concerned citizen may ask why the boycott.

My answer: I am a Deist, not a Christian. I belonged to the Corinth Baptist Church when I was an adolescent. However, thirty five years of domestic and international employment turned me away from the teachings as a youth. I believe all mankind are equal. There are no Chosen People.

Since medical retirement, I wrote two books explaining my views, especially regarding religion. To date, I received .98 cents in royalty. So, as the book sales went, so, did my attempts to bring the truth regarding those in our country that should be forced to identify themselves as foreign agents for the country of Israel failed.

With regards to my identification of the words, Foreign Agents, please find below four (4) criteria for mandatory registration as a foreign agent:

1. Engages in political activities for or in the interests of a foreign principal;

2. Acts in a public relations capacity for a foreign principal;

3. Solicits or dispenses any thing of value within the United States for a foreign principal;

4. Represents the interests of a foreign principal before any agency or official at the U.S. government.

My 2010 Election Platform was: (1) A single term as a U.S. Senator. (2) After swearing into office, I would ask the Chairman of the Ethnic Committees of the House of Representatives and the U.S. Senate to remove members of Congress with dual citizenship. (3) Ask the Drug Enforcement Agency to allow Commonwealth of Kentucky's Farmers, Merchants, and Citizens return Industrial Hemp as Kentucky's major revenue producing crop.

Lastly, I take exception to the clergy, Old Testament Christians, members of the United States Congress and individuals with dual citizenship subverting the United States of America. I will keep trying to enlighten our countrymen but life is short.

With respect, I remain,

BILLY RAY WILSON

CC To:

> Kentucky Attorney General
> Kentucky Secretary of State
> The White House
> LindaMilazzo.com

In Their Country

Independent (Write In) Candidate, Billy Ray Wilson's, Website review by an unknown writer and comments by 10 individuals.
The unknown writer emphasized "hating religion" in their early summary of my book writings. In truth, growing up in Laurel County in the 1950s, I was a baptized member of the Cornith Baptist Church, London, KY.
With entry [...]

Read the full article »

Write In Candidate

Reference the recent publication by Ms. Gloria Shur Bilchik, Subject: "$10,440 in South Carolina = $0 in Vermont" that examines each state's filing fee for a U.S. House of Representative and U.S. Senate Candidates plus if petition signatures of registered were required.
Ms. Bilchik's Kentucky summary was correct with the exception of petition signatures. Instead of [...]

Read the full article »

Candid Political Beliefs

There are a number of emergent actions that must be taken by the United States Congress to assure the physical and economic security of the United States of America. The failure to correct the treasonous actions by the Congress of the United States and the White House occupants since May 1948 has brought our nation (twice)to the brink of monetary bankruptcy, a continuous military or political turmoil in the Middle East, and Americans being denied their right for Life, Liberty and the Pursuit of Happiness.

As Americans, we have heard the saying the United States is the Melting Pot of all races, religions and ethnic cultures. To this, I am in agreement. However, individuals whose religions are Judaism and the literal believers of the Old Testament have led our nation away from being a nation where one's religion was a private relationship between a believer and their religious entity in to an aggressive political tool and subversive.

Moreover, Judea-Christians (Zionist) control national elections through their expertise in getting voters to the voting centers and their massive expenditures to the media. These methods have succeed in electing individuals to the U.S. Presidency since 1948 and the U.S. House of Representatives and U.S. Senate that are pro-Israel. For some reason the incumbent strays from supporting Israel, he or she becomes a one term incumbent. President Jimmy Carter and President George H.W. Bush are living examples of Zionist power.

As a Deist, I have the same belief as Thomas Jefferson and a number of our country's founders in that the Creator formed the universe but allows nature to control the day to day events of the universe. On earth, it is man that builds and multiplies in the physical form while mother nature cares for the earth's functions such as the weather, earthquakes, tornadoes, etc. I am an American first and foremost.

One may ask what is wrong with the election of an individual that is versed in the religious teachings that many older Americans believe were the foundation of our great nation?

The logical answer: the United States was not founded as a Theocracy Government but a Constitutional Republic. However, the worst case scenario, which exists, it that the Judea-Christian dominance elect American leaders that bide by the wishes of the religious community. To this end, the invasion of the sovereign nation of Iraq was, allegedly, the will of God according to former President George W. Bush. (Bush approved 30 billion dollars over the next 10 years prior to leaving office.) But, always a but, maybe the 1998 Iraq Liberation Act approved by Congress and signed by former President William Jefferson Clinton dictated the removal of Saddam Hussein. Could the approved liberation act be the true driving force for the illegal war?

Please do not take what I have written in the wrong way. I do not care what entity you worship or not worship. What I do take exception is the attempts by the religious community to pursue the advancement of their religion outside their homes or structures built for the purpose of religious studies and/or organized church functions in to the political affairs of our country.

There are more than 300 million Americans of which more and more each day are questioning the domestic and foreign policy actions in the name of God. We need to return to U.S. Constitution and Amendments thereto as the source of our government's foundation.

In reference to domestic policy, the internet columnist and pundits inform us actions of the U.S. Congress, in my cases, are not for Americans but hyphenated Americans. For example: (1) California has a greater diversity than most states except for maybe New York state. Too this end, California's Washington delegation are the protectors, both economic and physical security, of the state of Israel. (Representative Tom Lantos, CA, should have charged with TREASON because of this acts against the United States in favor of Israel.) The next level of representation would be to the Mexican community. No not the Hispanic American but Mexicans. The Black American community would follow the Hispanic American. The White Anglo-Saxon's environment are the least concerns of California politicians. (2) Arizona because of its large Hispanic population, members of Congress ignore the laws of the United States regarding immigration. Failure to side with the illegal residence or families of the illegal would mean the loss of their Congressional seat. (3) New York and New Jersey's politicians are in step with the California delegation. (4) Florida's Congressional delegation caters to Zionist and individuals of Cuban ancestry. The national delegations need to be replaced with Americans that understand the dictates of the U.S. Constitution. The United States belongs to all Americans, not just Zionist.

As a United States Senator, one term, I will seek to force on the Senate floor, acts that bring about secure borders and common sense immigration polices that would allow Mexican workers in to the United States.

There would be legislation that would force those employers that hire Mexican laborers to pay for their stay in the United States including all medical bills and school taxes. A child born in the United States would not receive an automatic American citizenship as the individual was a contracted worker, not an immigrant to the country.

Yes, the Commonwealth has its share of illegal individuals but not to the amount our state's judicial system can not manage, should the state desire.

The true danger to our state's employment and health care system are the influx of individuals from outside the Commonwealth and, of course, our generational welfare recipients.

Kentucky's generational welfare situation could easily be corrected but to do so would require the election of state officials that would rebuke the religious community. God has not and will not provide monetary instruments, health care, education, etc..

Kentuckians pay for married and single women to become pregnant. Following delivery, the state pays for milk and other baby essential products for the child. Next comes assistance in paying for baby sitters. Oh, of course, too many of the women are receiving some type government monetary subsistence and quite probably a Medicaid card. (From observation, one find the mothers of many children on welfare: smoke, take drugs, drink alcohol, take vacations to the Bahamas, Dollywood, etc.)

Why not teach sexual educations in school and distribute birth control devices at schools, county medical facilities and private doctor offices. The adult will exist at or below poverty level. The child will be mentally abused by having to eat free meals at school and/or the school provide back pack of food for the weekends. A child knows their environment.

Oh, I'm not letting the father off the hook. The best way to solve this problem is for a judge to order the father whether married or out of wedlock to care for their child. If the economy is in a depression or recession, suggest to the father to enlist into the military or some other government employment program. The child should receive a well rounded environment.

As a well versed individual of the international community, I know of no member country in the United Nations that persecutes an individual or individuals because of their religious beliefs. Yes, if the individual or individuals create domestic turmoil by their claim they are God's Chosen People or their God is greater than the God of the majority, then naturally, the host government must take action.

In London, Kentucky, Jewish leaders have established a shelter for the transients and a relocation office to assist in their movement to Israel or occupied Palestine. Naturally, while they are in the tri-county area they receive some type of federal monetary subsistence. Some even take jobs away from the indigenous Kentuckian.

Right away a reader may say Wilson is a racist, anti-Semite or some other demeaning word. To this situation, the following is a well researched conclusion regarding the Hebrews (Jews) of Palestine and Mesopotamia to the Jews of New York City, Los Angeles, Miami:

1. Jew is a term to identify a person whose religion is Judaism.

2. Jew is not a nationality.

3. History reveals the Hebrew tribe were one tribe of many of the Arab tribes in Palestine and Mesopotamia. (Recent DNA studies reveals the Palestinian and the Israeli (Hebrew) came from the same paternal lineage.)

4. There was never a sovereign state of Israel until 1948. Yes, there were two Kingdoms, Samaria and Judea, claimed to be governed by the Hebrews. However, the true power was the Roman Empire. (During his time in power, Israeli Prime Minister Sharon always made reference to Samaria and Judea. Never did he call the former kingdoms – Israel.)

5. Jesus' Mother Mary was allegedly a Hebrew which by Jewish custom made Jesus a Hebrew (Jew). His race would still be Arab.

6. From the days of the alleged Abraham the Hebrew (Jew), the Jew traveled from one land area to another for whatever the reason without regard to the owner of the land. (Such was the Hebrews transgression a plant was named the Wandering Jew.) While in the occupied area, they never assumed the nationality of the host country but instead remained a Hebrew (Jew).

7. Zionism is the belief that individuals whose religion is Judaism are God Chosen People. As God's People there must be a country established for Jews.

8. According to religious teaching, the God of Abraham is the God for Jews, Christians, and Muslims. Too me, this is confusing and frustrating. Confusing in that how can, say for instance, Christians ask God to Bless America, Jews ask God to destroy the Palestinians, and the Muslims ask God to move Jews from Palestine. Frustrating in that Americans and the indigenous of the Middle East are dying and being injured in the name of a God who wears three hats.

9. For a few minutes let us examine terrorism. For those individuals that take the Old Testament literally let us look at:

A. The mythical figure Moses allegedly told his sons, family members, and fellow Jews to go into Canaan (Palestine) and kill all human life, except for virgins, and occupy their land in the name of the God of Moses. The virgins were to be returned to Shiloh.

B. The alleged actions of a Jewish woman named Esther, Mordecai's cousin, who married the Persian King Ahasuerus. For a period of time, King Ahasuerus did not know his wife was Jewish until because of an order by the King to kill all Jews Esther came forward. The order was rescinded. (This incident is but one that identifies the cruelty, if true, by the different Jewish tribes and Persians. Today, we see the opposite in the Middle East. Jews wants the United States military to attack which would lead to an all out war so the state of Israel can posses their nuclear inventory and occupy more Arab land, even maybe going into Iran.)

C. In 1967, the Israeli Defense Forces (IDF) attacked their Arab neighbors to acquire more land, water resources, access to the sea, etc. During their attacks, IDF attacked the USS Liberty on station in international waters with by air and sea forces. The Liberty had to be salvaged, U.S. personnel were killed and wounded. There was no provocation by the United States Ship. (President Lyndon B. Johnson recalled Navy carrier aircraft launched to support the Liberty while she was under attack.)

D. President Ronald Reagan dispatched U.S. Marines to Lebanon in the 1980s following the invasion of Lebanon by Israeli Defense Forces. When the U.S. became active with military action against the Druze and other Lebanon tribes, the U.S. Embassy Compound was attacked resulting in the killing and wounding of a large number of U.S. Marines and other personnel assigned.

E. The aerial attack on the United States on September 11, 2001 was the results of United States unlimited support of the occupation of Palestine by the Israeli and at the time, U.S. Forces stationed in the Kingdom of Saudi Arabia. Osama bin Laden, an extremely religious and wealthy Saudi national and his Arab brothers, declared war on the United States.

Bin Laden alerted the White House to his organizations pending actions. The civilian targets were the Jewish areas of New York City, the structure housing the armed forces leadership, the Pentagon, and the Capitol of the United States housing the U.S. Congress. Had Bin Laden's attack succeed, President Bush could have succeeded, where his great grandfather and other Wall Streets executives failed, in a coup attempt against President Franklin D. Roosevelt.

On May 1, 2010, Mr. Faisal Shahzad, a naturalized American was suspect in a possible act of terrorism against the United States. He was born into a wealthy Pakistani family. His father was a Vice Air Marshall (two star U.S. Air Force General) in the Pakistani Air Force. After retirement for the Pakistani Air Force his father was a senior member of the International Civil Aviation Organization in Pakistan. Mr. Shahzad lived the life of a westerner with the best education and employment opportunities.

Based upon my knowledge of the Pakistani elite and their personal conviction of the Afghanistan and Iraq Wars, plus the occupation of Palestinian land, I do not believe Mr. Shahzad intended to explode a weapon in a Jewish section of New York City.

He voiced to his captors and the news media, his concern for NATO drones killing innocent citizens in Afghanistan and Pakistan. Apparently, Mr. Shahzad knew of the purchase of Israeli manufactured drones by NATO forces in Afghanistan that are used against Arabs of the region. (Israeli Americans departed the United States as they did in the 1920s and 1930s for Israel or Palestine. In Israel or occupied Palestine, they are starting up new corporations and manufacturing facilities that should have been built in the United States.)

And, it is my understanding, Mr. Shahzad voiced his concern and anger over our country's support for the country of Israel. Sadly, Mr. Shahzad failed to understand, the American news media is a subversive faction in the United States. His words regarding Israel will not be available nationally for Americans to read or observe.

F. In 1998, the Jewish controlled Congress approved the Iraq Liberation Act, which was signed by President William Jefferson Clinton, to remove Saddam Hussein from his position as President of Iraq. (Congress nor the President of the United States have to power to remove a head of state per the U.S. Constitution. Action on the Iran Liberation Act by Congress is forthcoming.) President George W. Bush ordered U.S. Forces to invade Iraq in March 2003. No Declaration of War by Congress. Jews win, the American people loose.)

10. Let us examine the origin of the three major religions in the world: Judaism, Christianity, and Islam.

Judaism was the first religion to be written naming the God of Abraham and stating Jews were God's Chosen People. Christianity followed with greater success. Emperor Constantine 1, the Great, became a Christian and made Christianity the religion of the Holy Roman Empire. To further the knowledge of Christianity, he ordered a number of Bishops to convene and write a Holy Bible. This was done.

Here we have two religions with the same God of Abraham. Of note, the Jews claim to be God's Chosen People. Christianity believes that no one can enter the Kingdom of Heaven without first believing in Jesus Christ as their personal savior.

Multiple hundreds of miles away from Jerusalem in Mecca and Medina, Arabia, an Arab name Mohammed, with a rich wife and equally rich Jewish friend, received visions which ordered him to write the Koran. The Koran was written but contained much of the same literature as the religious book of the Jews and Christians. The Koran stated there was only one God and that God was Allah.

The Koran became the Bible of the Arabs, who became known as Muslims, which was the religion of the Middle East countries and a large number of European countries. Through murderous wars, Muslims were forced from many European nations, Muslims returned to the Middle East with some exception. The Balkans in Europe have a strong Muslim population.

With regards to the religious community I take exception to prayers, by Jews, Old Testament Christians, and/or whomever for the world to be destroyed once Jews return to Jerusalem. Likewise, Muslims have a similar mythical belief about the return of a Muslim leader which will bring about the end of the world. However, too me, the destruction of the earth and the return of a religious leader to govern the world is just a myth. But, what really makes me angry is the transfer of wealth from individuals in the United States to the State of Israel and Zionist politicians. This action has kept our nation at war or in some type hostile action since 1948 all in the name of Israel.

During the periods when religions were colliding in the Middle East, including the failed Kingdom of Samaria and Kingdom of Judea, Hebrews began to migrate to eastern Europe, Turkey, and then to the Americas and other lands. To this end, the occupation of tribal lands and/or squatting in another's land came to a head in pre-World War II Germany and World War II. The pause in the Wandering Jew is over.

The Hebrew now calling themselves Jews became prosperous in Germany and elsewhere in Europe but would not accept the nationality of the host country. In Germany with the rise of the National Socialist German Worker's Party (1933-1945), Jews were asked to help the government to pay their war debt to the Allied Powers and rebuild Germany. (World War I damages.) The Jews refused.

The government of Germany offered Jews permission to leave Germany to whatever country would accept them. Many went to Palestine where they killed the Palestinian people and took their land. However, once Germany began to loose the war, Jews were forced to wear a star on their chest identifying themselves as Jews.

Following the defeat of the German military, U.S. Forces liberated a number of Concentration and Labor camps. These controlled environment facilities housed individuals the German government felt were responsible for domestic unrest and TREASON against the Third Reich. (Many of the same type people causing domestic upheaval in the United States today.)

Fast forward 65 years to a different continent and a new country – North America and the United States of America. Regretfully, the change of geographical locations didn't change the mind set of the Jewish people.
They retained their God's Chosen People status and, for example, in the United States they refuse to become Americans. They choose to be called Jews as if Judaism was a nationality.

After being elected, the first task will be to address the members of the Senate and the Vice President of the United States that our county is the United States of America. Our system of government is a Constitutional Republic. Following the address, if the President of the Senate allows, I will read my resolution regarding citizenship and immigration.

Let us look at citizenship:

1. To be a citizen of the United States of America you must be born in the United States of America, naturalized through the U.S. Immigration and Naturalization Service, and for children of Americans overseas on contract employment with a United States Company and/or a members of the U.S. Military, U.S. State Department, etc. The overseas American must only register the child with the United States Embassy's Consular Office.

2. The United States will no longer give citizenship to foreign nationals that come to the United States for the purpose of commerce. Our citizenship is not for sale.

3. Members of the legislative shall not have the power to award American citizenship because an overseas bank guard stopped the destruction of Jewish bank records. Special citizenships will not be approved without a voice vote by both houses of Congress.

4. No individual of any religion may enter or depart the United States of America without a passport and visa. No special status will given to any nationality because of their religious status.

5. Individuals whose religion is Judaism may not repeat may not be identified as Jews instead of Americans nor for any action of record or favorable employment by the United States Government will be awarded to a Jew based on their religion. Judaism is a religion, not a nationality.

6. The United States State Department will only allow the manpower of a foreign embassy to exceed a logical staff manning. (It has been reported the Israeli Mission to the United States has a larger staff than the largest nations with U.S. Missions.)

Immigration can easily be resolved:

1. Companies and/or individual seeking to hire a Mexican national for hire must submit a request to his or her state government's employment service. If the position can not be filled by an American, the state's unemployment office will contact the Mexican Government Unemployment Service. When and if a Mexican nationality is found that qualifies for the position, the Mexican Government will provide the necessary documentation for that individual or individuals to enter the United States.
After arrival at the employees destination, the employer will process the employee in accordance with Homeland Security Directives.

The employer will be responsible for the health and welfare of his employee. This means the employer will provide housing, food or allowance, transportation to and from work, and wages in according to U.S. Laws governing minimum wages. Also, the employer will be responsible for any health care of said employee. Should an employee be female, she will be made aware the birth of a child in the United States will not automatically granted citizenship.

2. The United States State Department shall not issue travel visa, employment visa, educational visa, etc to any repeat any foreign national alleging religious persecution.

3. The United States State Department shall not issue Passports for Americans of dual citizenship seeking travel to the Middle East. (Jews in the United States are known to be members of Mossad, Israeli Secret Service, that use their American citizenship to spy for the state of Israel.

There are three Americans of dual citizenship presently in an Iranian jail charged with spying for Israel. Another example, made in to the movie "Munich." Dual citizenship Americans were using the United States as a safe haven for their families while they used the United States as a staging area for covert operations against Arab targets. (Rich and powerful Jews in the United States funded the covert operations.)

And, on May 1, 2010, an American of Pakistani ancestry, a dual citizen American, allegedly attempted to create mass destruction in a Jewish section of New York City. Another example on why the U.S. State Department should terminate and refuse to issue any passport to a naturalized American, including Jews, that wish to remain as a resident of their former homeland.

Returning to my Senate office, I will write and dispatch a letter to the U.S. Drug Enforcement Agency asking them to issue a permit for the University of Kentucky to raise hemp as a test for its marketability and growth in the Commonwealth. I was informed some months past by a member of Kentucky's Agriculture Department, UK was waiting on the citing permit. (Kentucky farmers have grown HEMP for decades but due to the abilities of the HEMP plant, large corporations had the plant outlawed. We the people will overturn their efforts and bring the billion dollar market to Kentucky.)

Hemp production would be Kentucky back on her feet. Jobs for all.

A lot of Americans, including Kentuckians, are complaining about the National Health Plan. However, I am not one. My reasoning is that all Americans must have health care options of themselves and their family members, if any. The mandated health care program would require all, except a few, to have this care which would in effect force the dishonest among us to heads up to their responsibilities. It is not mine and your responsibility to maintain the health of any American that is physically and mentally able to do a day's work.

Abortion: The Federal Government, per the U.S. Constitution, has no say to the abortion question. Abortion is a state's right question.

Post Service: Section 8, paragraph (7) of the United States Constitution reads: To establish post offices and post roads. My response to the current policy of deactivating the London Regional Postal Service and transferring the service to the Lexington Post Office is a mistake.

The problem with the reduction of mail processing, in my opinion, is dishonesty, mismanagement, religion, and lack of pride in one's work.

As a frequent user both a my residence and at the postal office, I can state, without question, too many employees at the post office have a five day week employment mentality.

Either the employees do not want to work the weekends or the postal service refuses to pay the additional charge for working weekends and nights. Another major problem is now that our region has a large Jewish population, religious holidays become a problem for both the mail handlers and the route personnel. By taking off from work in observant of their holiday, the workers remaining on duty create a delay in the distribution to the rural route customers.

And, recently, the ACS supervisor spoke to a postal supervisor responsible for route and city distribution regarding delays in processing mail which produced late arrivals at their destinations. Allegedly, the mail supervisor told the ACS person that two of his mail handlers wanted to go deer hunting.

Moreover, from observations and questioning, we learned the postal union allows workers to build up hours of work time, for example, in a janitorial or like position. This allows the person to take off from work on what should be a normal work day without charge to their leave bank. (From my government experience, the positions cited would probably be deleted.)

Not all reading this paper may agree with me but as quoted the U.S. Constitution states Congress is responsible for post service. Therefore, it is my belief the postal service should be returned to the Federal Executive Branch as a Cabinet Position. My reasons:

1. Postal services are too important for both city and rural citizens. To this end, with a company, United States Postal Service, whose work ethic is mandated by a union this is unacceptable.

2. A union mandated postal service is a Clear and Present Danger to the United States.

3. Postal service should be available seven days per week. This would allow Americans a smooth and proficient flow of communications. Weekend stoppage hinders the movement of mail vital to the sender. Not all Americans, especially in the rural areas, are computer proficient or even own a computer.

4. During a true emergency, the union worker would, in my opinion, not suffer the possible wrath of mother nature or man made hardships to deliver correspondence so vital to the health and welfare of our citizens.

Congress can fund the postal service. Cut out support to the terrorist state of Israel and pork projects of too many members of Congress.

Firearms. Without question Americans have the unquestionable right to possess and sale firearms. It is not the weapon that kills or harms one, it is the handler of the weapons. (The problem with gun ownership lies with, once again, the dishonest in our nation.)

As a Vietnam era disabled veteran, I may be the only former enlisted man in the United States Senate. My tenure would be the first as most Senators and members of the U.S. House of Representatives were military officers, to the best of my knowledge. But, as an enlisted person, many avenues for grievance or knowledge of opportunities available the war veteran, were not available. To this end, let us address those military members that served in Cambodia, Laos, and Thailand during the Vietnam era.

For the unfamiliar, air bases in Thailand were the logistic bases for U.S. Forces early in the Vietnam War. The port of Bangkok and Sattahip on the Gulf of Thailand were overwhelmed with logistics for Vietnam and our secret war in the Kingdom of Laos. The Don Muang Thai Military Airbase and the Bangkok International Airport shared runways. This made these runways one of the busiest in the world.

Moreover, through these ports and airfields, the U.S. shipped the toxic defoliation fifty gallon drums of Agent Orange, Agent Blue and the other deadly Agents. In turn, these toxins were shipped up-country and to South Vietnam via military air, military surface, and contract Thai surface transportation. Without saying, safety and health precautions were never at the top of the list of things to do or watch out for.

Regarding the Agent series, these toxic fluids were used in Cambodia, Laos, Thailand and South Vietnam. Individuals handling the toxins were told that you could consume, for example Agent Orange, without any health dangers. We found out the truth too late.

Besides learning of the true toxic damage to our bodies and our children, the Department of Veterans Affairs has a ruling that unless those of us that served in Cambodia, Laos, and Thailand were assigned "Boots on the Ground" in the Republic of South Vietnam our claims for Diabetes Mellitus Type II and COPD – Asbestos/Agent Orange are denied.

And, of course, the veterans of the Gulf War, Iraq, and Afghanistan will face similar administrative hurdles from the Department of Veteran for future health claims as they get order and the poisons mature.

In the Senate, I will assure the true military disabled veteran that I shall be on their side whether on the Senate Floor or in the Committees. Also, after my actions against Israel, I will attempt to end our military conflict in Iraq and Afghanistan.

My fellow Kentuckians, reports from medical professionals and the news media are reporting children are being born in Iraq with three heads, a nose on their forehead and many, many other deformities from a parent's contact with depleted Uranium rounds and other toxic military equipment used by our forces in Iraq.

The reader may say so what. The what is that our servicemen were subjected to environments never envisioned by the national guardsmen, reservist and other forces. The American military man/woman bodies immunizations do not have immunity against bacteria and other ill health factors founds in the sands and water of Iraq.

On my watch, U.S. Troops will not fire a weapon at another individual in a hostile manner unless the U.S. Congress has declared war on an enemy of the United States of America and that individual is a hostile member.

Former President Thomas Jefferson warned Americans against alliances with foreign nations and/or organizations. Examples would be the Southeast Asia Treaty Organization (SEATO), North Atlantic Treaty Organization (NATO), the United Nations and the Socialist Country of Israel.

The United Nations has accomplished a lot in the international community. Polio no longer exist as a enemy of man, the international airways are safe to travel from one country to another, and a number of actions that have been helpful to mankind. But, there is always a but, the United States, Great Britain and France have made void the ideal of equity in foreign policy and the human rights of certain peoples. In 1947, the United Nations ruled that the city of Jerusalem would be administered by the United Nations. In 1967, the United Nations ordered Israel to return to its pre-1967 borders. Israel's violations go on and on because the United States is controlled by Zionist.

NATO took our nation to the Korean War and the war in the Balkans. SEATO took us to the Vietnam War.

And, throughout his political life, Jefferson stressed the separation of Church and State. In March 2003, President George W. Bush ordered U.S. Forces to invade the sovereign nation of Iraq. Bush told several world leaders "God told him to remove Saddam Hussein."

Jefferson envisioned the United States being an agriculture producing nation. He knew we could feed the world and that migration from the farms to large cities would pose social and monetary problems for government.

The warning of President Jefferson to print our own money and not allow a private banking institute control our economy, in my opinion, is responsible for the murder of President Abraham Lincoln and President John F. Kennedy as both wanted to eliminate the FEDERAL RESERVE BANK.

My fellow Kentuckians, the Declaration of Independence and the U.S. Constitution are sources of my actions in the United States Senate. I am an American.

I look forward to any questions and comments.

Contact Me

I look forward to hearing your comments, questions or concerns.

Billy Ray Wilson
209 Autumn Drive
London, KY 40744

(606) 862-2847 | Phone
(606) 330-0124 | Fax

brwilson04@windstream.net | E-mail

COUNTY VOTES FOR BILLY RAY WILSON
U.S. SENATE RACE 2010

COUNTY	# VOTES	IDENTIFIED/ NOT IDENTIFIED
Laurel	2	Write-In
Jefferson	843	Billy Ray Wilson
Pike	1	Billy Ray Wilson
Allen	2	Billy Ray Wilson
Anderson	4	Billy Ray Wilson
Boone	2	Billy Ray Wilson
Bourbon	1	Billy Ray Wilson
Boyle	1	Billy Ray Wilson
Bullitt	1	Billy Ray Wilson
Calloway	1	Write-In
Campbell	1	Billy Ray Wilson
Leslie	7	Write-In
Russell	1	Write-In
Pulaski	11	Write-In
Franklin	13	Billy Ray Wilson
Fayette	17	Billy Ray Wilson
Metcalfe	1	Billy Ray Wilson
Grayson	10	Billy Ray Wilson
Woodford	19	Billy Ray Wilson
Washington	1	Billy Ray Wilson
Warren	1	Billy Ray Wilson

Trimble	6	Write-In
Taylor	16	Billy Ray Wilson
Scott	1	Billy Ray Wilson
Ohio	1	Billy Ray Wilson
Mercer	8	Billy Ray Wilson
Meade	1	Billy Ray Wilson
McLean	4	Billy Ray Wilson
Graves	4	Billy Ray Wilson
Greenup	4	Billy Ray Wilson
Hardin	8	Billy Ray Wilson
Harrison	4	Billy Ray Wilson
Hart	1	Billy Ray Wilson
Henderson	6	Billy Ray Wilson
Henry	3	Billy Ray Wilson
Hopkins	2	Billy Ray Wilson
Jessamine	2	Billy Ray Wilson
Johnson	7	Write-In
Knott	8	Write-In
Livingston	4	Billy Ray Wilson
Logan	4	Write-In
Lyon	3	Write-In
Madison	117	Write-In
Marion	15	Billy Ray Wilson
Marshall	5	Billy Ray Wilson
Martin	3	Write-In
McCracken	12	Billy Ray Wilson
Edmonson	1	Billy Ray Wilson

Crittenden	6	Billy Ray Wilson
Christian	2	Billy Ray Wilson
Mason	1	Billy Ray Wilson
Oldham	8	Billy Ray Wilson
Shelby	2	Billy Ray Wilson
Knox	3	Write-In
Kenton	2	Billy Ray Wilson

TOTAL COUNTIES FOR: 55
NUMBER OF VOTES: 1,214 ?????????????

NON-VOTE COUNTIES

| | IDENTIFIED |
| COUNTY | NOT IDENTIFIED |

ADAIR	WRITE-IN
BALLARD	BILLY RAY WILSON
BARREN	BILLY RAY WILSON
BATH	BILLY RAY WILSON
BELL	WRITE-IN
BRACKEN	BILLY RAY WILSON
BOYD	BILLY RAY WILSON
BREATHITT	WRITE-IN
BRECKENRIDGE	BILLY RAY WILSON
BUTLER	BILLY RAY WILSON
CALDWELL	BILLY RAY WILSON
CARLISLE	BILLY RAY WILSON
CARROLL	BILLY RAY WILSON
CARTER	WRITE-IN
CASEY	WRITE-IN
CLARK	WRITE-IN
CLAY	WRITE-IN
CLINTON	WRITE-IN
CUMBERLAND	WRITE-IN
DAVIESS	BILLY RAY WILSON
ELLIOTT	WRITE-IN
ESTILL	WRITE-IN
FLEMING	WRITE-IN
FLOYD	WRITE-IN
FULTON	BILLY RAY WILSON

GALLATIN	BILLY RAY WILSON
GARRARD	BILLY RAY WILSON
GRANT	BILLY RAY WILSON
GREEN	WRITE-IN
HANCOCK	BILLY RAY WILSON
HARLAN	WRITE-IN
HICKMAN	BILLY RAY WILSON
JACKSON	WRITE-IN
LARUE	BILLY RAY WILSON
LAWRENCE	BILLY RAY WILSON
LEE	WRITE-IN
LETCHER	WRITE-IN
LEWIS	WRITE-IN
LINCOLN	WRITE-IN
MAGOFFIN	WRITE-IN
MCCREARY	WRITE-IN
MENIFEE	WRITE-IN
MONROE	BILLY RAY WILSON
MONTGOMERY	BILLY RAY WILSON
MORGAN	WRITE-IN
MUHLENBURG	BILLY RAY WILSON
NELSON	WRITE-IN
NICHOLAS	WRITE-IN
OWEN	BILLY RAY WILSON
OWSLEY	WRITE-IN
PENDLETON	WRITE-IN
PERRY	WRITE-IN
POWELL	WRITE-IN
ROBERTSON	WRITE-IN
ROCKCASTLE	WRITE-IN

ROWAN	BILLY RAY WILSON
SIMPSON	BILLY RAY WILSON
SPENCER	BILLY RAY WILSON
TODD	BILLY RAY WILSON
TRIGG	BILLY RAY WILSON
UNION	BILLY RAY WILSON
WAYNE	WRITE-IN
WEBSTER	BILLY RAY WILSON
WHITLEY	BILLY RAY WILSON
WOLFE	WRITE-IN

TOTAL COUNTIES: 65

Independent (Write In) Candidate, Billy Ray Wilson's, Website review by an unknown writer and comments by 10 individuals

The unknown writer emphasized "hating religion" in their early summary of my book writings. In truth, growing up in Laurel County in the 1950s, I was a baptized member of the Corinth Baptist Church, London, KY.

With entry into the United States Air Force on 30 September 1960, my travel through military assignments took me to a number of countries. To this end, I studied the country's history, the people, and their religion.

In Korea, I never learned of a religion as a curfew existed and the population of contact were in the entertainment industry. In Thailand and Laos, the primary religion was Buddhist, the second was probably Catholic. The islands of the Philippines had several religions. I believe the primary religion was Catholic. The southern islands had a large population of Muslims. In the Kingdom of Saudi Arabia, Islam in the dominant religion; however, since 1952 other religions are allowed. (You can't go door to door to recruit converts.)

As a young adult, Bible stories taught did not correlate with history of the Middle East, National Geographic articles, and countless other publications. Over time, I became a Deist; however, I do not care what or who you worship.

While researching the extent of my campaign, I queried the Internet. To my amazement, I found two of the following comments:

GINA wrote: I am sure he had a copy editor who removed all references to "camel jockey" and "kikes."

GINA is terribly wrong. In my mother's home there were no vulgar names called. All people were welcome to visit and share a meal.

The names camel Jockey and kikes were learned from movies at the theater. In the air force and air force contractors, we attended classroom training on the history of a country to be assigned, their people and customs. No one under my supervision used the words nor would any supervisor I knew allow the use of such words.

Maybe, vulgar names, etc., may lie with Ms. Gina.

JUST ME wrote: "Hell, maybe his Laotian tour caused irreparable brain damage."

JUST ME is correct. I've been diagnosed with Post Traumatic Stress Disorder, progress followed by a psychiatrist, and prescribed two separate psych medications. I am angry and have anxiety.

Let us look at possible causes: In Laos I was the supervisor of the Air Attache's Command & Control

Center. I was on duty 12 -14 hours per day with 2-3 hours of duty in the wee morning hours. We were responsible for all USAF and indigenous air strikes in Laos. Any search & rescue missions were acted upon by us and any besieged site needing combat air assistance contacted the Command Post.

Moreover, March 1969, three former U.S. Prisoner of War came from Hanoi via the International Control Commission aircraft to Vientiane. We worked until approximately 4:00 a.m. in the following morning assuring communications with family members was accomplished and whatever other tasks had to be accomplished. Returned around 8:00 a.m., the same morning to take money to the POWs, at the U.S. Ambassadors House, so they could purchase gifts for their family members.

On one occasion, I was ordered to replace a Combat Controller at a Forward Operating Base, LS-108, bordering the Plane de Jares. U.S. Mission and indigenous forces were attempting to retake the area from the North Vietnamese. Within few hours of myself and the five or six other enlisted (aircraft mechanics, bomb loaders, and weapons maintenance) personnel departing the site, Communist Forces attacked the site.

Had we been there, I would not be writing this paper. Following my tour at LS-108, a U.S. Army Captain was killed and his Army Sergeant wounded at the USAID Compound in the village of Moung Soui.

The last American pilot, Raven Jackson, in Laos was killed on December 24, 1972. (I gave the scheduled controller off to be with his friends and I worked his shift.) Jackson called me early in the morning airborne from the Vientiane Airport enroute to the LS-20A area.

Early afternoon, Raven Jackson encountered a A-7 midair. The A-7 pilot was captured but released during the release of Prisoners of War by North Vietnam.

According to the crew of the ON-The-Scene Search and Rescue operations, the Ravens body feel from the aircraft on to a field of high grass. A trail was spotted leading to the point of the Raven's impact with the earth.
Oh, my career stress factor gets worse. I was assigned to the Joint Casualty Resolution Center, Nakhon Phanom Royal Thai Air Base. Our mission was to make physical search of crash and incidents sites in Cambodia, Laos and Vietnam to recover remains. Days not in the field were spent reading volume's of TOP SECRET and other classified documents from international sources and from who knows where they originated.

What did these documents tell us?

Communist forces shot an American in the back of the head. An American was dropped on punji sticks and killed. A Navy Lieutenant was hung by his arms from the ceiling of a room. A Major in the U.S. Force was beaten to death with a fan belt because he would not bow down to the Cuban Fidel and North Vietnamese entering his cell. Day after day, you read where your fellow Americans were killed in an illegal war.

Now that we addressed illegal wars. Let us go back in time to 1998. This was the year, the Congress of the United States of America wrote and sent to the U.S. President for signature, the 1998 Iraq Liberation Act.

The Liberation Act funded and charged President William Jefferson Clinton to commit an act of war. The act was to removed Saddam Hussein as Iraqi Head of State.

President Clinton didn't bite. He did order additional missile and bombing strikes but not invasion.

Enter President George W. Bush and Vice President Richard Cheney. The World Trade Center and Pentagon were attacked by U.S. Air Carriers. The aircraft were, allegedly, hijacked by 19 Want To Be Saudis. A fourth aircraft crashed in a vacant field in Pennsylvania farm country.

This Air Operations Superintendent, along with physics, engineers, firemen, and a long list of other specialty vocations declare the Saudi's could not have accomplished the alleged attack without assistance from someone or some agency inside the government of the United States.

If elected, I will seek President Obama's assistance in ordering an investigation into the September 11, 2001 aerial attack on the United States. Within this period, I will also ask the Ethnic Committees of the U.S. Senate and U.S. House of Representative to remove, with prejudice, members of Congress that maintain dual citizenship.

Moreover, Vice President of the United States Joseph Biden should be either forced to resign from his office or denounce his Zionist standing.

The comments regarding my website and my words regarding individuals that use their religion to subvert the United States of America need to be addressed by the United States Justice Department and, if necessary, the U.S. Supreme Court.

A final note of interest, I learned today, Christian leadership in the birthplace of Christianity are concerned at the number of Christians departing. The exodus is due to the unending expansion of Jews into the lands of Palestine. Before long, the population will be once again, as in history, the Hebrew Arabs (Jews of all races) and the Arabs of Israel and surrounding Arab nations. Cousins, far removed, will murder and steal from each other as they have done for centuries.

The United States of America is a Constitutional Republic.

Political Reception
At
Spaulding University
Attendee:
Billy Ray Wilson
Independent (Write In) Candidate
United States Senate
Metro Disability Coalition Questions & Answers

1. In February 2010, an 18-member bipartisan commission was created by President Obama by Executive Order charged with reducing the federal deficit and controlling the growth of national debt. Given the spending cuts that would ensue as well as the significant impact of the current economic crisis on people with disabilities, who even in the best of times experience significant economic disparities, what is your position on maintaining the current level of services for the disabled?

Answer: One of my acts in the Senate will be to ask the Chairman of both the House of Representative and U.S. Senate Ethic Committees to remove/sanction/censor members of Congress who claim dual citizenship. By removing the traitor factor from our government, there would be no reason current levels or even increases can not be approved by the new American Congress.

2. There is an institutional bias in Medicaid that was deemed discrimination under the ADA in the 1999 Supreme Court Decision 'Integration Mandate' - Olmstead. What steps are you prepared to take to eliminate the barriers preventing the transition of funding to home and community based services for the disabled?

Answer: There will be no barriers. Every American is equal in the United States of America (Declaration of Independence). Too me every American has the right to reside in their own home or desired residential setting; when they reach their golden years of citizenship, disabled or whatever the reason. No one will be institutionalized. (My grandmother when she became ill with Cancer lived with us until her death.)

3. Accessible and affordable housing is a critical issue for the disabled community. Currently, restrictions on savings in Federal Financial Assistance Programs, the implementation of the Section 811 program to build or rehabilitate disability-specific, largely segregated housing, reduction of support for Section 8 Housing Vouchers that support integrated housing in the community and the failure to require that housing built or financed through at least three major tax subsides be accessible on a non-discriminatory basis are barriers to accessible and affordable housing for the disabled. What specific steps would you propose to address this issue?

Answer: I was not familiar with the Section 811 Program; whereas, I visited the Internet to inform myself. Regarding Section 8 Housing, I am quite familiar with that program as I once resided in the Kentucky Towers, Louisville, KY.

We, Americans, have many, many, many different life expectations. Some want a private life and no involvement in the hustle and bustle of every day activities. This group may work just enough to qualify for Section 8 Housing or a Habitat Home.

Another American may want the American dream of Life, Liberty and the Pursuit of Happiness but for whatever the reason, they are not employable for positions that would enable their American Dream.

Moreover, we have Americans that inside their Section 8 Housing, they live the American Dream while denying the true Section 8 eligible American their housing.

And, sadly, we have the American disabled military veteran who's only income is his or her Veterans Disability Pension and gratis Veterans Administration Health Care. To this end, from first hand knowledge, we learned many veterans require close monitoring of their activities.

With regards to one's monetary savings, I do not believe a Means Test should be applied when an American is truly disabled or unable, for whatever the reason, to own his or her own home and provide for their day to day lively-hood.

As a United States Senator, I would ask HUD and the Veterans Administration to become more aggressive in their release of funds to those that abuse subsidized housing. Funds will continue for those Americans that for whatever the reason are unable to attain the American Dream.

4. According to the National Council on Disability, the employment rate for the disabled in 2005 was 38% while it was 78% of all non-disabled. Given the current economic crisis, the situation is obviously much worse. Much of the problem can be attributed to negative stories about the ADA and people with disabilities. Would you be willing to sponsor public awareness initiatives such as public demonstration projects to confront this issue?

Answer: As a U.S. Senator, I would not have federal funds to prompt public awareness or demonstrations; however, I would use my position to seek donations for such a position as long as the donor did not assume, I would be politically obligated for the donation.

Moreover, on the floor of the U.S. Senate, I would be active in assuring the American, regardless of physical, mental, or monetary standing, would receive the benefits earned or required to live a honorable life.

Also, in the are of Vocational Rehabilitation, would you support a metric showing that disabled people were being placed in jobs commensurate with the level of training/education they received and not something far less in order to satisfy the 85% placement guidelines that currently govern reimbursement?

Answer. I do not believe in quotas and ego trips for administrators of government programs. If a person receives the training or education at the expense of the American taxpayer, then he or she should be afforded employment commensurate with said training/education.

5. Access to transportation is another crucial area of concern. Access to transportation in rural areas - especially Para transit - is the most pressing need according to a recent Senior Transportation 2010 Trends Report. Yet this is where the biggest service gap exist. What would you propose in the way of addressing this issue?

Answer: There is an existing transportation support system in Laurel County that provides transportation for the disabled and those of need. To this end, I have not read or heard of the need for more availability; however, if the need exists, I will support such an upgrade.

6. How does the Health Care Reform affect Medicare?

Answer: For a factual statement, I can not report. However, I, as an American, believe that President Barack H. Obama would not deny Americans of a favorable health plan. I am sure Medicare will continue to support those Americans qualified for said health care.

7. How will the budget affect Medicare?

Answer: I will seek to end the war of terrorism against nations that never harmed the United States. As a result, if successful, money will be available to provide health maintenance for all Americans. I, too, am a Medicare member.

8. With the current economic situation how will food stamps be controlled?

Answer: I didn't understand the question. Are there rumors of impending change to food stamp delivery?

If you are qualified for food stamps, then, you should be issued the stamps.

9. What kind of accountability do you purpose for Federal and State funds?

Answer: I do not understand the question; however, as a U.S. Senator I have a vote on the national budget; however, I have no legal input on state funds.

10. Under your administration would it be possible to appoint the elderly and disabled on boards and commissions?

Answer: Yes! Without a doubt.

11. What is your policy on immigration?

Answer: If you are not in the United States of America legally, then you should be deported.

How can Social Security and citizenship be verified?

Answer: Correct programs for both concerns are in place; however, as always, the administrators of the programs abuse the implementation of Presidential and Congressional Policies.

CANDID TALKING PAPER
Billy Ray Wilson
Independent candidate for U.S. Senate

There are a number of emergent actions that must be taken by the United States Congress to assure the physical and economic security of the United States of America. The failure to correct the treasonous actions by the Congress of the United States and the White House occupants since May 1948 has brought our nation (twice)to the brink of monetary bankruptcy, a continuous military or political turmoil in the Middle East, and Americans being denied their right for Life, Liberty and the Pursuit of Happiness.

As Americans, we have heard the saying the United States is the Melting Pot of all races, religions and ethnic cultures. To this, I am in agreement. However, individuals whose religions are Judaism and the literal believers of the Old Testament have led our nation away from being a nation where one's religion was a private relationship between a believer and their religious entity in to an aggressive political tool and subversive.

Moreover, Judea-Christians (Zionist) control national elections through their expertise in getting voters to the voting centers and their massive expenditures to the media. These methods have succeed in electing individuals to the U.S. Presidency since 1948 and the U.S. House of Representatives and U.S. Senate that are pro-Israel. For some reason the incumbent strays from supporting Israel, he or she becomes a one term incumbent. President Jimmy Carter and President George H.W. Bush are living examples of Zionist power.

As a Deist, I have the same belief as Thomas Jefferson and a number of our country's founders in that the Creator formed the universe but allows nature to control the day to day events of the universe. On earth, it is man that builds and multiplies in the physical form while mother nature cares for the earth's functions such as the weather, earthquakes, tornadoes, etc. I am an American first and foremost.

One may ask what is wrong with the election of an individual that is versed in the religious teachings that many older Americans believe were the foundation of our great nation?

The logical answer: the United States was not founded as a Theocracy Government but a Constitutional Republic. However, the worst case scenario, which exists, it that the Judea-Christian dominance elect American leaders that bide by the wishes of the religious community. To this end, the invasion of the sovereign nation of Iraq was, allegedly, the will of God according to former President George W. Bush. (Bush approved 30 billion dollars over the next 10 years prior to leaving office.) But, always a but, maybe the 1998 Iraq Liberation Act approved by Congress and signed by former President William Jefferson Clinton dictated the removal of Saddam Hussein. Could the approved liberation act be the true driving force for the illegal war?

Please do not take what I have written in the wrong way. I do not care what entity you worship or not worship. What I do take exception is the attempts by the religious community to pursue the advancement of their religion outside their homes or structures built for the purpose of religious studies and/or organized church functions in to the political affairs of our country.

There are more than 300 million Americans of which more and more each day are questioning the domestic and foreign policy actions in the name of God. We need to return to U.S. Constitution and Amendments thereto as the source of our government's foundation.

In reference to domestic policy, the internet columnist and pundits inform us actions of the U.S. Congress, in my cases, are not for Americans but hyphenated Americans. For example: (1) California has a greater diversity than most states except for maybe New York state. Too this end, California's Washington delegation are the protectors, both economic and physical security, of the state of Israel. (Representative Tom Lantos, CA, should have charged with TREASON because of this acts against the United States in favor of Israel.) The next level of representation would be to the Mexican community. No not the Hispanic American but Mexicans. The Black American community would follow the Hispanic American. The White Anglo-Saxon's environment are the least concerns of California politicians. (2) Arizona because of its large Hispanic population, members of Congress ignore the laws of the United States regarding immigration. Failure to side with the illegal residence or families of the illegal would mean the loss of their Congressional seat. (3) New York and New Jersey's politicians are in step with the California delegation. (4) Florida's Congressional delegation caters to Zionist and individuals of Cuban ancestry. The national delegations need to be replaced with Americans that understand the dictates of the U.S. Constitution. The United States belongs to all Americans, not just Zionist.

As a United States Senator, one term, I will seek to force on the Senate floor, acts that bring about secure borders and common sense immigration polices that would allow Mexican workers in to the United States.

There would be legislation that would force those employers that hire Mexican laborers to pay for their stay in the United States including all medical bills and school taxes. A child born in the United States would not receive an automatic American citizenship as the individual was a contracted worker, not an immigrant to the country.

Yes, the Commonwealth has its share of illegal individuals but not to the amount our state's judicial system can not manage, should the state desire.

The true danger to our state's employment and health care system are the influx of individuals from outside the Commonwealth and, of course, our generational welfare recipients.

Kentucky's generational welfare situation could easily be corrected but to do so would require the election of state officials that would rebuke the religious community. God has not and will not provide monetary instruments, health care, education, etc..

Kentuckians pay for married and single women to become pregnant. Following delivery, the state pays for milk and other baby essential products for the child. Next comes assistance in paying for baby sitters. Oh, of course, too many of the women are receiving some type government monetary subsistence and quite probably a Medicaid card. (From observation, one find the mothers of many children on welfare: smoke, take drugs, drink alcohol, take vacations to the Bahamas, Dollywood, etc.)

Why not teach sexual educations in school and distribute birth control devices at schools, county medical facilities and private doctor offices. The adult will exist at or below poverty level. The child will be mentally abused by having to eat free meals at school and/or the school provide back pack of food for the weekends. A child knows their environment.

Oh, I'm not letting the father off the hook. The best way to solve this problem is for a judge to order the father whether married or out of wedlock to care for their child. If the economy is in a depression or recession, suggest to the father to enlist into the military or some other government employment program. The child should receive a well rounded environment.

As a well versed individual of the international community, I know of no member country in the United Nations that persecutes an individual or individuals because of their religious beliefs. Yes, if the individual or individuals create domestic turmoil by their claim they are God's Chosen People or their God is greater than the God of the majority, then naturally, the host government must take action.

In London, Kentucky, Jewish leaders have established a shelter for the transients and a relocation office to assist in their movement to Israel or occupied Palestine. Naturally, while they are in the tri-county area they receive some type of federal monetary subsistence. Some even take jobs away from the indigenous Kentuckian.

Right away a reader may say Wilson is a racist, anti-Semite or some other demeaning word. To this situation, the following is a well researched conclusion regarding the Hebrews (Jews) of Palestine and Mesopotamia to the Jews of New York City, Los Angeles, Miami:

1. Jew is a term to identify a person whose religion is Judaism.

2. Jew is not a nationality.

3. History reveals the Hebrew tribe were one tribe of many of the Arab tribes in Palestine and Mesopotamia. (Recent DNA studies reveals the Palestinian and the Israeli (Hebrew) came from the same paternal lineage.)

4. There was never a sovereign state of Israel until 1948. Yes, there were two Kingdoms, Samaria and Judea, claimed to be governed by the

Hebrews. However, the true power was the Roman Empire. (During his time in power, Israeli Prime Minister Sharon always made reference to Samaria and Judea. Never did he call the former kingdoms - Israel.)

5. Jesus' Mother Mary was allegedly a Hebrew which by Jewish custom made Jesus a Hebrew (Jew). His race would still be Arab.

6. From the days of the alleged Abraham the Hebrew (Jew), the Jew traveled from one land area to another for whatever the reason without regard to the owner of the land. (Such was the Hebrews transgression a plant was named the Wandering Jew.) While in the occupied area, they never assumed the nationality of the host country but instead remained a Hebrew (Jew).

7. Zionism is the belief that individuals whose religion is Judaism are God Chosen People. As God's People there must be a country established for Jews.

8. According to religious teaching, the God of Abraham is the God for Jews, Christians, and Muslims. Too me, this is confusing and frustrating. Confusing in that how can, say for instance, Christians ask God to Bless America, Jews ask God to destroy the Palestinians, and the Muslims ask God to move Jews from Palestine. Frustrating in that Americans and the indigenous of the Middle East are dying and being injured in the name of a God who wears three hats.

9. For a few minutes let us examine terrorism. For those individuals that take the Old Testament literally let us look at:

A. The mythical figure Moses allegedly told his sons, family members, and fellow Jews to go into Canaan (Palestine) and kill all human life, except for virgins, and occupy their land in the name of the God of Moses. The virgins were to be returned to Shiloh.

B. The alleged actions of a Jewish woman named Esther, Mordecai's cousin, who married the Persian King Ahasuerus. For a period of time, King Ahasuerus did not know his wife was Jewish until because of an order by the King to kill all Jews Esther came forward. The order was rescinded. (This incident is but one that identifies the cruelty, if true, by the different Jewish tribes and Persians. Today, we see the opposite in the Middle East. Jews wants the United States military to attack which would lead to an all out war so the state of Israel can posses their nuclear inventory and occupy more Arab land, even maybe going into Iran.)

C. In 1967, the Israeli Defense Forces (IDF) attacked their Arab neighbors to acquire more land, water resources, access to the sea, etc. During their attacks, IDF attacked the USS Liberty on station in international waters with by air and sea forces. The Liberty had to be salvaged, U.S. personnel were killed and wounded. There was no provocation by the United States Ship. (President Lyndon B. Johnson recalled Navy carrier aircraft launched to support the Liberty while she was under attack.)

D. President Ronald Reagan dispatched U.S. Marines to Lebanon in the 1980s following the invasion of Lebanon by Israeli Defense Forces. When the U.S. became active with military action against the Druze and other Lebanon tribes, the U.S. Embassy Compound was attacked resulting in the killing and wounding of a large number of U.S. Marines and other personnel assigned.

E. The aerial attack on the United States on September 11, 2001 was the results of United States unlimited support of the occupation of Palestine by the Israeli and at the time, U.S. Forces stationed in the Kingdom of Saudi Arabia. Osama bin Laden, an extremely religious and wealthy Saudi national and his Arab brothers, declared war on the United States.

Bin Laden alerted the White House to his organizations pending actions. The civilian targets were the Jewish areas of New York City, the structure housing the armed forces leadership, the Pentagon, and the Capitol of the United States housing the U.S. Congress. Had Bin Laden's attack succeed, President Bush could have succeeded, where his great grandfather and other Wall Streets executives failed, in a coup attempt against President Franklin D. Roosevelt.

On May 1, 2010, Mr. Faisal Shahzad, a naturalized American was suspect in a possible act of terrorism against the United States. He was born into a wealthy Pakistani family. His father was a Vice Air Marshall (two star U.S.

Air Force General) in the Pakistani Air Force. After retirement for the Pakistani Air Force his father was a senior member of the International Civil Aviation Organization in Pakistan. Mr. Shahzad lived the life of a westerner with the best education and employment opportunities.

Based upon my knowledge of the Pakistani elite and their personal conviction of the Afghanistan and Iraq Wars, plus the occupation of Palestinian land, I do not believe Mr. Shahzad intended to explode a weapon in a Jewish section of New York City.

He voiced to his captors and the news media, his concern for NATO drones killing innocent citizens in Afghanistan and Pakistan. Apparently, Mr. Shahzad knew of the purchase of Israeli manufactured drones by NATO forces in Afghanistan that are used against Arabs of the region. (Israeli Americans departed the United States as they did in the 1920s and 1930s for Israel or Palestine. In Israel or occupied Palestine, they are starting up new corporations and manufacturing facilities that should have been built in the United States.)

And, it is my understanding, Mr. Shahzad voiced his concern and anger over our country's support for the country of Israel. Sadly, Mr. Shahzad failed to understand, the American news media is a subversive faction in the United States. His words regarding Israel will not be available nationally for Americans to read or observe.

   F. In 1998, the Jewish controlled Congress approved the Iraq Liberation Act, which was signed by President William Jefferson Clinton, to remove Saddam Hussein from his position as President of Iraq. (Congress nor the President of the United States have to power to remove a head of state per the U.S. Constitution. Action on the Iran Liberation Act by Congress is forthcoming.) President George W. Bush ordered U.S. Forces to invade Iraq in March 2003. No Declaration of War by Congress. Jews win, the American people loose.)

   10. Let us examine the origin of the three major religions in the world: Judaism, Christianity, and Islam.

   Judaism was the first religion to be written naming the God of Abraham and stating Jews were God's Chosen People. Christianity followed with greater success. Emperor Constantine 1, the Great, became a Christian and made Christianity the religion of the Holy Roman Empire. To further the knowledge of Christianity, he ordered a number of Bishops to convene and write a Holy Bible. This was done.

Here we have two religions with the same God of Abraham. Of note, the Jews claim to be God's Chosen People. Christianity believes that no one can enter the Kingdom of Heaven without first believing in Jesus Christ as their personal savior.

Multiple hundreds of miles away from Jerusalem in Mecca and Medina, Arabia, an Arab name Mohammed, with a rich wife and equally rich Jewish friend, received visions which ordered him to write the Koran. The Koran was written but contained much of the same literature as the religious book of the Jews and Christians. The Koran stated there was only one God and that God was Allah.

The Koran became the Bible of the Arabs, who became known as Muslims, which was the religion of the Middle East countries and a large number of European countries. Through murderous wars, Muslims were forced from many European nations, Muslims returned to the Middle East with some exception. The Balkans in Europe have a strong Muslim population.

With regards to the religious community I take exception to prayers, by Jews, Old Testament Christians, and/or whomever for the world to be destroyed once Jews return to Jerusalem. Likewise, Muslims have a similar mythical belief about the return of a Muslim leader which will bring about the end of the world. However, too me, the destruction of the earth and the return of a religious leader to govern the world is just a myth. But, what really makes me angry is the transfer of wealth from individuals in the United States to the State of Israel and Zionist politicians. This action has kept our nation at war or in some type hostile action since 1948 all in the name of Israel.

During the periods when religions were colliding in the Middle East, including the failed Kingdom of Samaria and Kingdom of Judea, Hebrews began to migrate to eastern Europe, Turkey, and then to the Americas and other lands. To this end, the occupation of tribal lands and/or squatting in another's land came to a head in pre-World War II Germany and World War II. The pause in the Wandering Jew is over.

The Hebrew now calling themselves Jews became prosperous in Germany and elsewhere in Europe but would not accept the nationality of the host country. In Germany with the rise of the National Socialist German Worker's Party (1933-1945), Jews were asked to help the government to pay their war debt to the Allied Powers and rebuild Germany. (World War I damages.) The Jews refused.

The government of Germany offered Jews permission to leave Germany to whatever country would accept them. Many went to Palestine where they killed the Palestinian people and took their land. However, once Germany began to loose the war, Jews were forced to wear a star on their chest identifying themselves as Jews.

Following the defeat of the German military, U.S. Forces liberated a number of Concentration and Labor camps. These controlled environment facilities housed individuals the German government felt were responsible for domestic unrest and TREASON against the Third Reich. (Many of the same type people causing domestic upheaval in the United States today.)

Fast forward 65 years to a different continent and a new country - North America and the United States of America. Regretfully, the change of geographical locations didn't change the mind set of the Jewish people. They retained their God's Chosen People status and, for example, in the United States they refuse to become Americans. They choose to be called Jews as if Judaism was a nationality.

After being elected, the first task will be to address the members of the Senate and the Vice President of the United States that our county is the United States of America.   Our system of government is a Constitutional Republic. Following the address, if the President of the Senate allows, I will read my resolution regarding citizenship and immigration.

Let us look at citizenship:

    1. To be a citizen of the United States of America you must be born

in the United States of America, naturalized through the U.S. Immigration and Naturalization Service, and for children of Americans overseas on contract employment with a United States Company and/or a members of the U.S. Military, U.S. State Department, etc. The overseas American must only register the child with the United States Embassy's Consular Office.

2. The United States will no longer give citizenship to foreign nationals that come to the United States for the purpose of commerce. Our citizenship is not for sale.

3. Members of the legislative shall not have the power to award American citizenship because an overseas bank guard stopped the destruction of Jewish bank records. Special citizenships will not be approved without a voice vote by both houses of Congress.

4. No individual of any religion may enter or depart the United States of America without a passport and visa. No special status will given to any nationality because of their religious status.

5. Individuals whose religion is Judaism may not repeat may not be identified as Jews instead of Americans nor for any action of record or favorable employment by the United States Government will be awarded to a Jew based on their religion. Judaism is a religion, not a nationality.

6. The United States State Department will only allow the manpower of a foreign embassy to exceed a logical staff manning. (It has been reported the Israeli Mission to the United States has a larger staff than the largest nations with U.S. Missions.)

Immigration can easily be resolved:

1. Companies and/or individual seeking to hire a Mexican national for hire must submit a request to his or her state government's employment service. If the position can not be filled by an American, the state's unemployment office will contact the Mexican Government Unemployment Service. When and if a Mexican nationality is found that qualifies for the position, the Mexican Government will provide the necessary documentation for that individual or individuals to enter the United States. After arrival at the employees destination, the employer will process the

employee in accordance with Homeland Security Directives.

The employer will be responsible for the health and welfare of his employee. This means the employer will provide housing, food or allowance, transportation to and from work, and wages in according to U.S. Laws governing minimum wages. Also, the employer will be responsible for any health care of said employee. Should an employee be female, she will be made aware the birth of a child in the United States will not automatically granted citizenship.

2. The United States State Department shall not issue travel visa, employment visa, educational visa, etc to any repeat any foreign national alleging religious persecution.

3. The United States State Department shall not issue Passports for Americans of dual citizenship seeking travel to the Middle East. (Jews in the United States are known to be members of Mossad, Israeli Secret Service, that use their American citizenship to spy for the state of Israel.

There are three Americans of dual citizenship presently in an Iranian jail charged with spying for Israel. Another example, made in to the movie "Munich." Dual citizenship Americans were using the United States as a safe haven for their families while they used the United States as a staging area for covert operations against Arab targets. (Rich and powerful Jews in the United States funded the covert operations.)

And, on May 1, 2010, an American of Pakistani ancestry, a dual citizen American, allegedly attempted to create mass destruction in a Jewish section of New York City. Another example on why the U.S. State Department should terminate and refuse to issue any passport to a naturalized American, including Jews, that wish to remain as a resident of their former homeland.

Returning to my Senate office, I will write and dispatch a letter to the U.S. Drug Enforcement Agency asking them to issue a permit for the University of Kentucky to raise hemp as a test for its marketability and growth in the Commonwealth. I was informed some months past by a member of Kentucky's Agriculture Department, UK was waiting on the citing permit. (Kentucky farmers have grown HEMP for decades but due to the abilities of the HEMP plant, large corporations had the plant outlawed. We the people will overturn their efforts and bring the billion dollar market to Kentucky.)

Hemp production would be Kentucky back on her feet. Jobs for all.

A lot of Americans, including Kentuckians, are complaining about the National Health Plan. However, I am not one. My reasoning is that all Americans must have health care options of themselves and their family members, if any. The mandated health care program would require all, except a few, to have this care which would in effect force the dishonest among us to heads up to their responsibilities. It is not mine and your responsibility to maintain the health of any American that is physically and mentally able to do a day's work.

Abortion: The Federal Government, per the U.S. Constitution, has no say to the abortion question. Abortion is a state's right question.

Post Service: Section 8, paragraph (7) of the United States Constitution reads: To establish post offices and post roads. My response to the current policy of deactivating the London Regional Postal Service and transferring the service to the Lexington Post Office is a mistake.

The problem with the reduction of mail processing, in my opinion, is dishonesty, mismanagement, religion, and lack of pride in one's work.

As a frequent user both a my residence and at the postal office, I can state, without question, too many employees at the post office have a five day week employment mentality.

Either the employees do not want to work the weekends or the postal service refuses to pay the additional charge for working weekends and nights. Another major problem is now that our region has a large Jewish population, religious holidays become a problem for both the mail handlers and the route personnel. By taking off from work in observant of their holiday, the workers remaining on duty create a delay in the distribution to the rural route customers.

And, recently, the ACS supervisor spoke to a postal supervisor responsible for route and city distribution regarding delays in processing mail which produced late arrivals at their destinations. Allegedly, the mail supervisor told the ACS person that two of his mail handlers wanted to go deer hunting.

Moreover, from observations and questioning, we learned the postal union allows workers to build up hours of work time, for example, in a janitorial or like position. This allows the person to take off from work on what should be a normal work day without charge to their leave bank. (From my government experience, the positions cited would probably be deleted.)

Not all reading this paper may agree with me but as quoted the U.S. Constitution states Congress is responsible for post service. Therefore, it is my belief the postal service should be returned to the Federal Executive Branch as a Cabinet Position. My reasons:

1. Postal services are too important for both city and rural citizens. To this end, with a company, United States Postal Service, whose work ethic is mandated by a union this is unacceptable.

2. A union mandated postal service is a Clear and Present Danger to the United States.

3. Postal service should be available seven days per week. This would allow Americans a smooth and proficient flow of communications. Weekend stoppage hinders the movement of mail vital to the sender. Not all Americans, especially in the rural areas, are computer proficient or even own a computer.

4. During a true emergency, the union worker would, in my opinion, not suffer the possible wrath of mother nature or man made hardships to deliver correspondence so vital to the health and welfare of our citizens.

Congress can fund the postal service. Cut out support to the terrorist state of Israel and pork projects of too many members of Congress.

Firearms. Without question Americans have the unquestionable right to possess and sale firearms. It is not the weapon that kills or harms one, it is the handler of the weapons. (The problem with gun ownership lies with, once again, the dishonest in our nation.)

As a Vietnam era disabled veteran, I may be the only former enlisted man in the United States Senate. My tenure would be the first as most Senators and members of the U.S. House of Representatives were military officers, to the best of my knowledge. But, as an enlisted person, many avenues for grievance or knowledge of opportunities available the war veteran, were not available. To this end, let us address those military members that served in Cambodia, Laos, and Thailand during the Vietnam era.

For the unfamiliar, air bases in Thailand were the logistic bases for U.S. Forces early in the Vietnam War. The port of Bangkok and Sattahip on the Gulf of Thailand were overwhelmed with logistics for Vietnam and our secret war in the Kingdom of Laos. The Don Muang Thai Military Airbase and the Bangkok International Airport shared runways. This made these runways one of the busiest in the world.

Moreover, through these ports and airfields, the U.S. shipped the toxic defoliation fifty gallon drums of Agent Orange, Agent Blue and the other deadly Agents. In turn, these toxins were shipped up-country and to South Vietnam via military air, military surface, and contract Thai surface transportation. Without saying, safety and health precautions were never at the top of the list of things to do or watch out for.

Regarding the Agent series, these toxic fluids were used in Cambodia, Laos, Thailand and South Vietnam. Individuals handling the toxins were told that you could consume, for example Agent Orange, without any health dangers. We found out the truth too late.

Besides learning of the true toxic damage to our bodies and our children, the Department of Veterans Affairs has a ruling that unless those of us that served in Cambodia, Laos, and Thailand were assigned "Boots on the Ground" in the Republic of South Vietnam our claims for Diabetes Mellitus Type II and COPD - Asbestos/Agent Orange are denied.

And, of course, the veterans of the Gulf War, Iraq, and Afghanistan will face similar administrative hurdles from the Department of Veteran for future health claims as they get order and the poisons mature.

In the Senate, I will assure the true military disabled veteran that I shall be on their side whether on the Senate Floor or in the Committees. Also, after my actions against Israel, I will attempt to end our military conflict in Iraq and Afghanistan.

My fellow Kentuckians, reports from medical professionals and the news media are reporting children are being born in Iraq with three heads, a nose on their forehead and many, many other deformities from a parent's contact with depleted Uranium rounds and other toxic military equipment used by our forces in Iraq.

The reader may say so what. The what is that our servicemen were subjected to environments never envisioned by the national guardsmen, reservist and other forces. The American military man/woman bodies immunizations do not have immunity against bacteria and other ill health factors founds in the sands and water of Iraq.

On my watch, U.S. Troops will not fire a weapon at another individual in a hostile manner unless the U.S. Congress has declared war on an enemy of the United States of America and that individual is a hostile member.

Former President Thomas Jefferson warned Americans against alliances with foreign nations and/or organizations. Examples would be the Southeast Asia Treaty Organization (SEATO). North Atlantic Treaty Organization (NATO), the United Nations and the Socialist Country of Israel.

The United Nations has accomplished a lot in the international community. Polio no longer exist as a enemy of man, the international airways are safe to travel from one country to another, and a number of actions that have been helpful to mankind. But, there is always a but, the United States, Great Britain and France have made void the ideal of equity in foreign policy and the human rights of certain peoples. In 1947, the United Nations ruled that the city of Jerusalem would be administered by the United Nations. In 1967, the United Nations ordered Israel to return to its pre-1967 borders. Israel's violations go on and on because the United States is controlled by Zionist.

NATO took our nation to the Korean War and the war in the Balkans. SEATO took us to the Vietnam War.

And, throughout his political life, Jefferson stressed the separation of Church and State. In March 2003, President George W. Bush ordered U.S. Forces to invade the sovereign nation of Iraq. Bush told several world leaders "God told him to remove Saddam Hussein."

Jefferson envisioned the United States being an agriculture producing nation. He knew we could feed the world and that migration from the farms to large cities would pose social and monetary problems for government.

The warning of President Jefferson to print our own money and not allow a private banking institute control our economy, in my opinion, is responsible for the murder of President Abraham Lincoln and President John F. Kennedy as both wanted to eliminate the FEDERAL RESERVE BANK.

My fellow Kentuckians, the Declaration of Independence and the U.S. Constitution are sources of my actions in the United States Senate. I am an American.

I look forward to any questions and comments.

With respect, I remain,

Billy Ray Wilson

BILLY RAY WILSON
Independent Candidate for the United States Senate

Dear Americans of our beloved Commonwealth,

Sorry, for taking to so long to let you know our election results: 1,214 votes.

I want to thank each and everyone that voted for not just me but the Constitution of the United States of America.

My days of on the road politics are over but not my hopes for a better future for our nation. (My mind wants to keep going but the physical body is say no.) However, let us find a General Dwight David Eisenhower that will step up and once again make our nation, the country envisioned those brave colonist in 1776.

Speaking of on the road. I always believe the Commonwealth was the most beautiful and had the possibility of being the most influential state of the United States and my political travels confirmed that belief.

My goodness, the Commonwealth has waterways, outstanding highways, airports with 24/7 capability, farm areas for livestock to graze and family farmers to grow agriculture products to sustain the nation. Fossil fuel reserves but, equally important, the Commonwealth has the environment for the production of bio-fuels, wind turbine electricity, and on and on.

The only factor we need to succeed is the will of the young people to learn and adhere to the spirit and vision of the

Declaration of Independence and the dictates of the United States Constitution. The founders of this nation never promised anything free to anyone. One must earn their way through life and/or be supported by a love one.

Moreover, the type of government turned over to the people by our founders was a Republic. This means we, the citizens, of the United States are the government. We do not need any outside force to build and keep our nation.

On a political note, I confirmed outside forces are active in the nation's political forum; therefore, the following lengthy narrative addresses foreign involvement in the affairs of the United States of America.

Subject: Unregistered Foreign Agents for the Socialist Country of Israel

An article in Thursday, November 4, 2010, Herald-Leader revealed, from post election poll canvassing, four out of five Kentuckians voted for Doctor Rand Paul because of the religious political adds ran by both Attorney General Jack Conway and Dr. Rand Paul.

Attorney General Conway questioned why Rand Paul, as a student, would join a fraternity outlawed by the school's administrator? Dr. Rand Paul's team finessed Conway's statements in to a negative message for Kentucky's religious zealots.

November 5, 2010 Herald-Leader Cartoonist, Joel Pett, continued the Aqua Buddha conversation, with a cartoon depicting Senator Mitch McConnell, Senator-Elect Rand Paul walking down a red carpet to pay homage to a large bag of the Almighty D'Allah. A statue of the Aqua Buddha was situated on the carpet.

In the same Herald-Leader publication, there was a similar text article written by Mr. Henry Olsen at the American Enterprise Institute, Washington, DC. The subject: Troubling trends: "GOP wins with whites, less educated." However, within the text, Mr. Olsen contends "Working-class whites voted Republican primarily because they intensely dislike President Barack Obama . The GOP captured about 10 percent of blacks' support and a third of Hispanics."

Yes! President Obama did very poorly in the Commonwealth, especially within Kentucky's 5th U.S. Congressional District, during the 2008 Presidential Election. (The votes he did receive came from the better educated and informed citizen.) The reason for the inherent prejudice, in my opinion, may be rooted from hand me down religious beliefs taught during the U.S. Civil War era.)

For the record, the United States of America is not a Judeo-Christian (Theocracy) Governed Nation. Our form of government is a Constitutional Republic. Individuals, in my opinion, that spread untruths should be charged with subversion and, equally important, have to register as a foreign agent for the Socialist Country of Israel.

Moreover, Article 6, paragraph 3, of the United States

Constitution, informs Americans: no religious prerequisite mandatory to seek public office. (Actions by Attorney General Conway and Dr. Rand Paul were a slap at the generational religious beliefs of the people of Kentucky.)

Equally frustrating, in my opinion, too many Kentuckians participate in national and state elections as if the elections were a sporting event. For example, the Republican Party is the University of Kentucky Wildcats. The Democratic Party is the Louisville Cardinals. (Or vice versa.)

And, there are Kentuckians who would vote for the political party's mascot. Existing difficulties, such as our country's engagement in to two illegal wars, allowing members of Congress to have dual citizenship and the Vice President of the United States acknowledgment he was a Zionist, didn't register. The party came first.

And, too many have forgotten the functions of the three branches of the U.S. Federal Government. For example, the President of the United States is the administrator of laws, regulations, policies that are designed to keep our nation safe, our people employed via creating a well regulated commerce and an expeditious flow of U.S. Mail.

The United States Congress, U.S. House of Representatives and U.S. Senate, is responsible for the oversight of the U.S. Presidential Administration to assure the dictates of the U.S. Constitution are adhered.

Should an enemy force physically attack the United States or our territories, it is the responsibility for the U.S. Congress to

Declare an Act of War. (The President has the authority to deploy forces for a short period of time until such time Congress can convene to either approve funds for the war or deny funding. If funding is denied, then military forces will return to the barracks.) In no instance must the U.S. Congress, through legislative action, fund and force the U.S. President to remove a sovereign nation's Head of State. (Reference: 1998 Iraq Liberation Act.)

Nor, should U.S. Congressional lawmakers flood the White House and the media with letters and news releases complaining about the Obama administration's unprecedented scolding of Israeli Prime Minister Binyamin Netanyahu. (As usual, the Israeli Government approved the building of more illegal settlements on Palestinian land. President Obama wants to end the on-going, since May 1948, genocidal actions by the Hebrew Arabs (Jews) against their Palestinian Arab cousins. Zionist in our country do not want peace.)

Going further, Senator Sam Brownback, R-KS, not only berated the President because of the administration's support for a two state solution in Palestine but wants to move the U.S. Israeli Embassy to Jerusalem. (A clear violation of United Nations Resolutions.) Per the U.S. Constitution, the President of the United States is the administrator of U.S. Foreign Policy. Yes, Congress does have an oversight responsibility.

The Justices of the U.S. Supreme Court are charged per the U.S. Constitution to debate and deliver a majority vote on laws and/other actions set forth by the Presidential Administration and/or the U.S. Congress. (Too me allowing U.S. Corporations and other entities to flood the political area with unlimited and unaccounted funds are not Constitutional. So went the 2010 National Election.)

Of note, November 5, 2010, the national news media reported that Republican leader, the Honorable Mitch McConnell, declared President Obama must be a one term President. The GOP had too many policies President Obama was blocking. (I suspect two of the policies were the invasion of Iran and allowing the Israeli to proceed with the plans for a Greater Israel.) President John F. Kennedy and Attorney General Robert Kennedy attempted to rein in Israeli expansion but failed due to the murder of the President Kennedy and Attorney General Kennedy.

As an American retired (disabled) military veteran, I sought the Office of the United States Senate being vacated by the Honorable Jim Bunning (R-KY). I chose to seek the office as an Independent Candidate because my country is more than a sporting event or belief that an unproven religious entity is more important than the sovereignty of the United States of America.

Both the Democrat and Republican Parties have their own agendas for our country's resources. The agendas do not concern the American people but special interest groups and corporation wealth.

Following months of correspondence, visits to the Laurel County Clerk's Office, and related political activities, I was listed on the Commonwealth's U.S. Candidate List as a Write In candidate. However, to my knowledge, no national news agency identified me as a qualified Senatorial Candidate nor following the election, post votes received.

Not understanding why at least one national news media did not identify my candidacy, I sent an e-mail to Diane Sawyer, ABC News, and Katie Couric, CBS News. I received a formatted e-mail response from ABC, No response from CBS

The failure of the national news media recognize my candidacy really floored me as they recognized the former unemployed Army/Air Force individual (Mr. Alvin Greene) from South Carolina. To Greene's credit he did win the Democratic Primary as a candidate for the U.S. Senate.

More frustrating was the report, Mr. Greene had only paid the large dollar amount to become a candidate for the U.S. Senate in South Carolina. Allegedly, he had no web site, campaign literature or other entities associated with a political campaign. (Mr. Greene is awaiting a court date in response to a felony charge.)

Regarding my campaign, I established a website; www.americanforussenate.com. Campaign business cards were purchased. A few yard signs were distributed, Talking Papers written and distributed identifying my platform. Two separate inserts were distributed throughout the state via the Lexington Herald-Leader Newspaper. I attended a number of political forums at key cities within the Commonwealth. I accepted no donations. For the London Community, I ran a political advertisement for one month at London's Regency Cinema.

My e-mail address, brwilson04@windstream.net, phone number, 606-862-2874, and fax number, (606) 330-0124) became personal and campaign numbers.

Reviewers of my website (13 comments) found my website (Hot Wire) well organized but my platform offended them. I was labeled a racist, an anti-Semite, crazy, and ignorant. One particular person accused me of using vulgar names for different ethnic groups.

Regarding the charge of racist: I am an American that adheres to the words of the Declaration of Independence and the U.S. Constitution. We are all Americans. There are no hyphenated Americans in the United States. We are all Americans.

The charge of anti-Semitism was not unusual. It is a known fact I regard the illegal nation of Israel as an affront to humanity. Hebrews Arabs (Jews) have been killing any and all that might obstruct Zionist goal of a greater Israel for centuries. To this end: 1. Judaism is a religion, not a nationality or citizenship legally in the international community except for the Socialist Country of Israel. 2. Personally, I do not care if your religious entity is your right big toe. Build a altar, put a picture of your toe on coffee mugs or whatever, I do not care. However, when religion dictate the political decisions of this nation, I take exception and will at the peril of death attempt to protect my country.

I may be crazy and ignorant but my love is for the United States of America. I have no loyalty except to the United States.

Now to vulgarism. I will be the first to acknowledge there was a time in my life that I did use a lot of profanity and some today. However, never in my life did I use vulgar names to identify an ethnic group. The words the reviewer used, I learned from watching movies.

Most Kentucky news media have been bias and/or non-attentive. To my knowledge only the Lebanon Enterprise identified me as opposing the Democrat and Republican candidates. The Sentinel-Echo, my hometown newspaper, provided each Senatorial Candidate with the same amount of column space and photograph to identify themselves and their platform.

Friday morning, November 5, 2010, the Sentinel-Echo Newspaper, London, KY, published the November 2, 2010, election results via precincts.. To my surprise, I received two votes: One from an Absentee Machine; the other from Absentee Mail. Regarding other votes, I can not say there were any; however, friends informed me they did vote for me. I know of one confirmed vote. I voted for myself. Where is that vote?

After reading the election print-out provided by the Sentinel-Echo, I contacted Kentucky's Secretary of State and Election Council. I was informed there were 10 counties not reporting; however, votes should be posted within a few days.

With the election over, I scanned the Internet to find any national media confirmation of my candidacy. To date, none exists. A concerned citizen may ask why the boycott.

My answer: I am a Deist, not a Christian. I belonged to the Corinth Baptist Church when I was an adolescent. However, thirty five years of domestic and international employment turned me away from the teachings as a youth. I believe all mankind are equal. There are no Chosen People.

Since medical retirement, I wrote two books explaining my views, especially regarding religion. To date, I received .98 cents in royalty. So, as the book sales went, so, did my attempts to bring the truth regarding those in our country that should be forced to identify themselves as foreign agents for the country of Israel failed.

With regards to my identification of the words, Foreign Agents, please find below four (4) criteria for mandatory registration as a foreign agent:

1. Engages in political activities for or in the interests of a foreign principal;
2. Acts in a public relations capacity for a foreign principal;
3. Solicits or dispenses any thing of value within the United States for a foreign principal;
4. Represents the interests of a foreign principal before any agency or official at the U.S. government.

My 2010 Election Platform was: (1) A single term as a U.S. Senator. (2) After swearing into office, I would ask the Chairman of the Ethnic Committees of the House of Representatives and the U.S. Senate to remove members of Congress with dual citizenship. (3) Ask the Drug Enforcement Agency to allow Commonwealth of Kentucky's Farmers, Merchants, and Citizens return Industrial Hemp as Kentucky's major revenue producing crop.

Lastly, I take exception to the clergy, Old Testament Christians, members of the United States Congress and individuals with dual citizenship subverting the United States of America. I will keep trying to enlighten our countrymen but life is short.

With respect, I remain,

Billy Ray Wilson

BILLY RAY WILSON

Cy To: Kentucky Attorney General
        Kentucky Secretary of State
        The White House
        LindaMilazzo.com

UNIFORMED CITIZENS

While reading the Herald-Leader's, May 31, 2010, OPINIONS section column under the title "Kentucky's Fallen Patriots" I cursed and thought, "don't they know the truth?"

The news media loves to write about death and any other tragic event that will sale newspaper. But, they will not write about why, for example, the Marines are assigned to Helmand Province, Afghanistan or why our country invaded Iraq.

Before I go any further, I want to emphasize the wars in Iraq and Afghanistan are not the product of President Barack H. Obama. The Bush/Cheney Administration are the fathers of the wars. Oh, past administrations may have contributed to the Bush/Cheney course of action but men of honor do not sell out their country and countrymen. They make the wrong - right.

From research, we find, in my opinion, U.S. covert and overt civilian/military operations in Afghanistan began during President Jimmy Carter's Administration. For example, on July 3, 1979, per internet communication, President Carter signed approval for U.S. support to opponents of the pro-Soviet regime in Kabul. This action, hopefully, would induce the Soviet Union to invade Afghanistan.

By mid to late 1980s, the U.S. wishing to increase regional influence requested assistance from the Royal Saudi Government to recruit an army of Saudis, Egyptians, and others into Afghanistan. Allegedly, the Saudi Government chose Osama bin Laden to lead the recruiting effort. His efforts were too successful. Among his recruits were individuals belonging to the Muslim Brotherhood, a regional fundamentalist group.

And, through bin Laden's efforts, coupled with the open-ended covert support of the United States Government and equal funds from Saudi Arabia, Afghanistan saw the departure of the Soviet Union's armed forces and administrators. However, unexpected results came from departure of the Soviets. Bin Laden's forces came to be known as Al Qaeda. The Afghanistan fundamentalist group became the Taliban.

For once, a Republican President, Ronald Reagan, and a Democrat President, Jimmy Carter, were instrumental in bringing about a results sought since the end of World War II. The collapse of the Soviet Union.

The General Secretary of the Soviet Communist Party was gone. The number of nations against the United States' Foreign Policy had been reduced. For example, former captive Caspian Sea states became free of their Soviet administrators. Three of the states, Azerbaijan, Kazakhstan, and Turkmenistan, immediately became "dreams answered" by the American Oil Companies. It was estimated there were 200 billion barrels of oil in the Caspian Sea area.

In 1997, the U.S. Congress passed a resolution declaring the Caspian and Caucasus region to be a "zone of vital American interests." (Congress violated the United States Constitution. Foreign Policy is the responsibility of the President of the United States. Congress has oversight authority, not meddling in international affairs.)

In December 1997, Unocal invited Taliban representatives to their corporate headquarters in Sugarland, TX to discuss a long sought pipeline project. They were later invited to Washington for meetings with the Clinton Administration. (August 13, 1996, Unocal and Delta Oil Co. of Saudi Arabia signed a memorandum of understanding to build a pipeline from Turkmenistan to Pakistan through Afghanistan. Pipeline construction was delay as it was a number of times due to armed hostilities in Afghanistan.)

In 1998, Richard Cheney, then the Chief Executive Officer of Halliburton oil services company stated: "I cannot think of a time when we have had a region emerge as suddenly to become as strategically significant as the Caspian."

February 28, 1998, Unocal's Vice President for International Relations addressed the U.S. House of Representatives. The official clearly stated "the Taliban Government should be removed and replaced with a government acceptable to his company. He argued that creation of a 42 inch oil pipeline across Afghanistan would yield a Western profit increase of 500% by 2015.

In 1998, Osama bin Laden, the former recruiter and leader of Arab fighters, against the Soviet occupation of Afghanistan declared War on the United States. His reasons for the declaration was the stationing of American military forces in the Kingdom of Saudi Arabia and the occupation of Palestine by the government of Israel. (At one time, a Royal Saudi motto for the King of Saudi Arabia read "the Protector of the three Holy Mosques." The three were: Mecca, Medina and the Dome on the Mount. Mecca and Medina are in Saudi Arabia. The Dome on the Mount is in Jerusalem. Today, the motto only includes Mecca and Medina.)

August 7, 1998, allegedly terrorist linked to Osama bin Laden bombed two U.S. Embassies. One in Nairobi, Kenya and the other Dar es Salaam, Tanzania. (Similar scenario some years past. The late Congressman Tom Lantos wanted money for the Jewish Community in Kenya and lo and behold, terrorist fired a ground to air missile against an Israeli Charter Aircraft leaving a Kenyan airport. The terrorist laid out the weapons on a blanket arranged ever so careful for the world to find. Israel was awarded the money to install flare systems on their aircraft to avoid being struck by heat seeking missiles.)

August 20, 1998, President Clinton order 75-80 cruise missile attacks on Afghanistan and Sudan.

August 22, 1998, the British Broadcasting Corporation reported the U.S. Government and Osama bin Laden exchanged warnings over the missile attacks.

July 4, 1999, President Clinton signed an executive order freezing U.S. held Taliban assets and prohibiting trade plus other transactions with Afghanistan.

October 15, 1999, the United Nations Security Council imposed sanctions on the Taliban Government and demanded the Taliban "turn over" Osama bin Laden

October 12, 2000, the U.S.S. Cole was attacked in the Yemeni port of Aden.

January - February 2001. Immediately upon taking office, the Bush Administration met with Taliban representatives in Washington, DC, Berlin, and Islamabad to discuss the proposed pipeline.

May 15, 2001, a U.S. official delivered a message to the Taliban that "Either you accept our offer of a carpet of gold, or we bury you under a carpet of bombs."

July 2001, A former Pakistani Foreign Secretary was told that military action against Afghanistan would go ahead by the middle of October.

October 7, 2001, Military operations against Afghanistan began.

The United States removed the Taliban from power but prior to operational control of the entire country, the U.S. changed their point of interest to Iraq and invaded same. Osama bin Laden, Al Qaeda and Taliban leaders escaped.

The situation is Afghanistan is the same in some ways as the Vietnam War. The Afghans, are independent and religious people, do not want foreigners to have a say in their government. However, Afghanistan is worse than Vietnam because Vietnam was a colony of the French Government. There were no religion dictates in the French Colony; whereas, there was an open, free for all society. The difference in foreign policy is that the United States was in Vietnam because of membership to the South East Asia Treaty Organization. Afghanistan is for oil.

Now my response to the cited Herald-Leader column:

Regarding the Marine deaths in Helmand Province, I have strong reservations about writing the truth as the truth will hurt many if the Herald-Leader prints this letter. The truth is the province had to be secured to allow for the construction of an oil pipeline and mining operations in the region.

During the Soviet occupation, Soviet specialists discovered huge oil and gas reserves in north Afghanistan. A pipeline was constructed to supply gas to the Soviet Union. Recently, an Afghanistan government official allegedly told the press "we have 330 idle or damaged oil and gas wells all drilled by the Soviet Union."

Moreover, FSU (Russian Oil & Gas Company) Oil and Gas Statistic Yearbook 2009, available on the internet, reports: Afghanistan has a large deposits of ferrous and non-ferrous metals, including iron, copper and rare ores such as used in the air and space industry. Iron ore was estimated at over 110 mm tons. Uranium was found in Helmand Province. Of course gold, silver, and other precious metals were discovered.

To secure Helmand Province, the U.S. Marines built Camp Leatherneck Marine Based in Helmand Province. (Afghans call the area where the base was built, "desert of death.") The base is a 443 acre reservation that will eventually be the home of 55 helicopters and other aircraft. Allegedly, the project is the largest of it's kind in a combat environment.

The pipeline project is called TAPI, for Turkmenistan, Afghanistan, Pakistan, and India. The four countries signed the pipeline deal in April 2008. Pipeline construction was scheduled to being in 2010 and completed in 2014 at an estimated cost of $7.6 billon dollars. The Asian (ADB) Development Bank is financing the deal. However, agreements have been reached that will decrease or eliminate influence on the project by the largest donor, the United States of America.

Yes, Helmand Province was secured and will be maintained by the lives of Americans whether U.S. Military or civilian contractors. Following Helmand Province, the Marines are preparing to move against Kandahar, Afghanistan, a city of 391,190 to 450,000, in a country with a population of 28,150,000. However, what will make the task of conquest even more difficult is that not all the people of Kandahar consider themselves to be or hold allegiance to the Taliban.

For the uniformed, the Taliban are primarily from the Pashtun tribes, along with volunteers from nearby Islamic countries such as Uzbeks, Tajiks, Chechens, Arabs, Punjabis and others. Their religious sect is Sunni, the same as the Kingdom of Saudi Arabia, but with harsher enforcement of Islamic laws.

It is said the Soviet invasion and the civil war that followed the Soviet's withdrawal influenced Taliban ideology. The teachers that were teaching the future generations were barely literate and did not include teachers learned in Islamic law and history. Often being refugees, the students had no education in mathematics, science, history or geography. Even worse, if possible, they had no traditional skills of farming, herding, or handicraft-making, nor even knowledge of their tribal and clan lineages.

Straying a bit, I remember a Saudi student being awarded a medal while I worked in Saudi Arabia. The student memorized the entire Koran but I doubt if he or she knew the meaning of the words memorized. But, wait, the situation in our country is not much better. We have school districts in the different states that are deleting guidance by former President Thomas Jefferson regarding Church & State Separation and adding Creationism to their school's curriculum.

Both school systems teach hate and mistrust. However, the greatest tragedy is that in our country the highly degreed politicians, lobbyist, cabinet members are illiterate in the way of life in the many different countries of the Middle East. So, each Presidential Administration in an attempt to appease the money lenders and their respective political parties send off Americans to die or to be maimed for corporate profit or a fabricated GOD.

The country of Afghanistan will never in my lifetime or yours conform with the so-called goals of U.S. administrations. You must remember the past years in the United States where women did not have the right to vote, women had to sit on one side of the church and men the other, women could not be the head of a household, and, still to date, there are individuals questioning civil rights in the United States. Leave Afghanistan alone. Bring our troops home.

Now for Iraq.

Iraq is easier to understand. In 1998, the Congress of the United States produced the Iraq Liberation Act (An Iran Liberation Act also exists) which was signed by President William Jefferson Clinton. The act released funds and provided guidance for President Clinton to remove President Saddam Hussein of Iraq. President Clinton didn't bite.

President George W. Bush and Vice President Richard Cheney assumed the leadership of the United States and free world amid intense controversy. President Bush had a history of being absent without leave from his Air Force Reserve Squadron and was berated as not having the qualifications of being President. Vice President Cheney was a man with multiple years of government and private sector expertise and of questionable character.

Bush would have the title of President while Cheney would subvert our republic and government administrator.

Subversion of our republic came early as one might remember from President Bush's statement the U.S. Constitution was nothing but a God Damn piece of paper. Vice President Cheney, in my opinion, as director of a national air defense exercise was contributory to the aerial attacks on September 11, 2001. Spain and other countries have questioned the pre and post attack scenarios.

And, history notes another Bush, Prescott, along with money lenders from Wall Street were mentioned in an attempted coup against President Franklin D. Roosevelt in similar periods of history. Marine Corps General Butler foiled the attempt.

To accomplish an act of war against Iraq, the Bush Administration had to have three other Zionist controlled states, Great Britain, France and Germany, as partners to sway the international community that Iraq was a threat to United States and Europe. March 2003, the United States, Great Britain and others invaded Iraq.

There were no weapons of mass destruction found. The downed American Gulf War pilot was not withering away in an Iraqi prison. No fixed or rotary winged chemical delivery system was found. Al-Qaeda was unwelcome in Iraq. Iraq didn't attempt to purchase yellow cake. King Hussein of Jordan informed the U.S. there were no Weapons of Mass Destruction. One lie after another. The lies weren't new to those of us that had up close and personal knowledge of the Middle East.

Without a doubt, a major factor for the invasion of Iraq was for money lenders to control Iraqi oil reserves and access of the oil to the international market. The actions were not uncommon as the United States and Great Britain overthrew the government of Iran in the 1950s to gain access to Iran's oil. (Great Britain changed energy modes from coal to oil to fuel their naval vessels and expanding air forces.)

And an equal deploring factor to the invasion of Iraq was the saying that all roads to Jerusalem went through Baghdad. The Hebrew Arab has always been threatened by the population of the land area presently known as Iraq.

Without a Saddam Hussein Government in Iraq, Israel could rob, steal and murder the indigenous population of Palestine in their efforts to build a greater Israel as envisioned by their first Prime Minister.

Yes, the U.S. Military is a voluntary armed force. The military person swears an oath near the flag of the United States that he or she will defend the U.S. Constitution against all enemies both foreign and domestic. The military member understands that he or she are obligated to obey the orders of the President of the United States or the officers appointed over them. However, the Uniform Code of Military Justice provides that a military member may disobey an order if he or she believes said order is unlawful.

As a military person, one does not want to be in a situation where he or she refuses to obey an order of those appointed by the President or the President him or her self. The Airman, Coast Guardsman, Marine, Sailor, and Soldier expects members of Congress to adhere to the United States Constitution in that Congress must make a Declaration of War prior to the nation going to all out war. No where in the Constitution does it authorize American forces deployed to secure fossil fuel, engagement in a religious crusade, support an alliance such as the Southeast Asia Treaty Organization or the North Atlantic Treaty Organization.

I am not sure if my fellow Kentuckians are aware of what I have written but, if not, they need to be. I know of no one that wants his or her family member to be killed or wounded in hostile actions against an opposing enemy force but one can understand if, in fact, there was an enemy force, at our door step, determined to overtake the United States of America. There have been none since the end of World War II.

The American military person is a son, daughter, husband, wife, uncle, aunt, etc., that volunteered to serve this great nation. They come from all states, territories, and Washington, D.C. They care not the race, gender, religion, economic status, education level of their comrade as when blood spills on a battle field and runs together, the color is the same.

I have attempted, with my lack of understand English Grammar, to covey the need to return to the dictates of the United States Constitution. To do so could eliminate the corrupt and treasonous politicians, not Americans, that sit in the halls of Congress. There has been no declaration of war since

World War II, yet Congress has ordered the U.S. President to deploy American forces for greed, religion, alliances, and ego. It is time to stop.

In November 2010, take a good look at the candidates. Vote and elect only Americans. (Those with access to the internet can read the dollar amount received by each member of the U.S. House of Representatives and the U.S. Senate.)

I thank you for your attention.

Billy Ray Wilson

Billy Ray Wilson
209 Autumn Drive
London, KY 40744-7071
(606) 862-2847 phone
(606) 330-0124 fax
brwilson04@windstream.net e-mail
www.americanforussenate.com website

UNAMERICANS

During the past few weeks, the Herald-Leader, the Times-Tribune and the Sentinel-Echo newspapers published articles which should have awakened the silent majority to the realization the United States is no longer a nation envisioned by our founders or even the 1950s under the Eisenhower administration. For example, in an issue of the Herald-Leader, there was a personal interest article relating to a son's memory of his father and his father's quotes. One such quote "NAZI is the worst," I found offensive.

How could NAZI be the worst? NAZI is not a person, a fabricated God, or the World Zionist Organization. The acronym NAZI stood for the first word in the German name of the National Socialist German Workers Party. It was a political party founded by a group, most angry veterans, following the end of World War I. Adolph Hitler joined the group in 1919 and became party leader.

In 1930, Adolph Hitler was appointed German Chancellor. From 1933 to 1945, the NAZI Party, with Adolph Hitler, governed the German Fatherland.

For truths sake, the NAZI Government brought Germany from the brink of economic disaster to the most powerful industrial nation and military power in Europe. However, on the domestic front, Hitler's government inherited a people's assimilation adversity.

The adversity came in two ethnic groups, Jews and Gypsies. Both parties sought autonomy from German Government while accepting the benefits of the state. Peaceful, helpful methods were used for a number of years to bring about assimilation and/or assistance in migrating. For example, with the initiation of

Zionism, the German government recommended Jews migrate to the land of Palestine. Many accepted the governments assistance and migrated as did many Jews from the international community, including the United States.

However, when the German military began to loose forward mobility in World War II, tactics were changed in regards to the Jewish and gypsy population. Biased historians called this period "Holocaust."

In 1945, combined forces of the allied nations defeated the Third Reich's armed forces. Adolph Hitler killed himself. Germany's domestic adversity was not resolved but in fact spread to the Soviet Union and the United States.

In the United States following World War I, the Zionist movement came alive in Detroit, Michigan, Wisconsin, and, of course, other national locations with a large population of individuals whose religion was Judaism. However, in Washington, DC, the first act of treason occurred during my lifetime.

May 1948, President Harry S. Truman, a Zionist Christian, recognized the announcement by Jewish terrorist and settlers in Palestine that Israel was a sovereign nation. Within hours, the Supreme Soviet Leader Joseph Stalin recognized Israel's statehood status.

Moreover, as a disabled military veteran with six years Middle East expertise and one that keeps abreast of events in the Middle East, I can state without question, every American military death or injury in the Middle East since 1948 is in some way connected to the illegal occupation of Palestine.

Moving forward to 1998, it was this year that Osama bin Laden, a

Saudi national who assisted U.S. advisors and Afghan fighters defeat the Soviet Military in Afghanistan, informed the U.S. Government that he an his organization, Al-Qaeda, were at war with the United States. His stated reasons were the presence of U.S. Military in the Kingdom of Saudi Arabia and the United States' unlimited support to the occupiers of Palestine - Israel.

September 11, 2001, allegedly, Al-Qaeda launched a successful aerial assault on the Twin Towers in New York City, the Pentagon, and a failed attack on the United States Capitol. Several thousand individuals were killed with an unknown number of persons with deep mental scars.

Within the past couple of months, the United States has received more warnings of future attacks and one act of terrorism by a naturalized American. The terrorist suspect, a man from a wealthy military family in Pakistan, told investigators he was a Muslim soldier. He also was adamant regarding drone attacks in Pakistan and the United States' military action in Afghanistan and Iraq. Of course U.S. support of Israel was addressed.

What does it take for Americans to wake up and replace the government of the United States? Jews control Congress. The U.S. Vice President is a Zionist. The news media is complicit in that they cater to a fabricated God when reporting news from the Middle East.

June 23, 2010, the U.S. Military Commander in Afghanistan was forced to retire because of his and his staff members comments regarding members from the White House. Also, without a doubt, the General's words some months past regarding our country's support for Israel surely upset our Zionist Vice President. (Those of us that have worked with the U.S. State Department and expertise in the Middle East know the United States can not win in

Afghanistan. Equally upsetting, Americans are being killed to secure areas for the building of a 7.6 billion dollar pipeline through southern Afghanistan which reportedly U.S. contributors are the main donors.

For the father and his son: The worst, in my opinion, are those individuals born or migrated to the United States that will not assimilate into the American population, as Americans, based upon mythical tale that the God of Abraham chose the Hebrew Arab as his Chosen People.

The United States of America is a republic governed by the people of the United States. There are no Royal Families. We have no established religion or supreme religious leader(s) that dictate our daily lives. A citizen can take employment and rise to whatever he or she desires and/or lie down for Americans to support. We have a voluntary armed force at the ready to defend our nation against all enemies both foreign and domestic. Most of all, we have no hyphenated Americans in the United States.

BILLY RAY WILSON
209 AUTUMN DRIVE
LONDON, KY 40744-7071
(606) 862-2847 PHONE

"THOSE THAT CANNOT LEARN FROM HISTORY ARE DOOMED TO REPEAT IT" George Santayna

Throughout history, great civilizations destroyed themselves by establishing a welfare system and administrating their governments following fabricated religion teachings. Religion and government do not mix.

I realize most Kentuckians from Kentucky's 5th U.S. Congressional District take the Old Testament and the New Testament literally based on hand me down religious teachings from their forefather. However, In truth and a matter of record, the supreme being and/or God, called upon by many Kentuckians, is based on a belief that Abraham (Abram) the Hebrew. an Arab from UR, Mesopotamia (Chaldees) that an unseen entity had spoken to Abraham a number of times.

For clarification, Abraham's God is the same God for those of Judaism, Christianity, and Islam; however, each religions God goes by a different name. So when one calls on God to support their country, the armed forces, etc. which hat is God wearing at the time of prayer?

For myself, I am overjoyed that one of our country's greatest president and one of the most literate of our founders, the honorable Thomas Jefferson, spoke through letters to the subject of separation of church and state. Mr. Jefferson's opinion was not based on his personal belief but first hand observations while he was Ambassador to France and his immense knowledge of world history. He knew the damage a state religion could inflict on a country and her people.

In the late 1770s & 1780s, Thomas Jefferson, Benjamin Franklin, James Madison, Thomas Paine, George Washington and many other prominent Americans delivered to the American people the Declaration of Independence and the United States Constitution. We became a nation of one people - Americans.

The Declaration of Independence was a listing of crimes against the colonist by the British Crown but more important announced to all that Americans were equal before their government and peers. (Then: taxation without representation. Now: War without representation.) The Constitution was a blueprint on how to build and administer a government of the people.

Moreover, each state and territory has their own state flag and motto, state bird, state flower, etc. Kentucky's state motto is: United We Stand. Divided We Fall. We see a frontiersman and a city dweller greeting each other in friendship. There are no clergyman or religious representation on the state flag.)

With a combined population of approximately 309 million individuals from all races, religions, and ethnic cultures; the United States is a nation where the President of the United States has to be born in the United States.

I suppose our founders believed the President would be a person of the people and love this country and, more so, believed the Chief Executive would die defending the nation against all enemies both foreign and domestic. Our founders were wrong. Belief in a fabricated religion set aside honor and loyalty.

Members of Congress and state officials, including state governor's may become representatives of the people without being born in the United States. However, they must be naturalized citizens.

Equally noteworthy, Article 6, section 3 requires both federal and state officials to give supreme allegiance to the United States Constitution. This section also rules there would be no religious affiliation required to hold federal office. The 14th Amendment applies the same non-religious ruling for state and local officials.

Greater still, the United States of America is a Constitutional Republic. For example, our country does not have royal families, a designated religion, or a caste system. The domestic (individual states) leadership of the United States is selected by individual voters at the ballot box and nationally by the Electoral College.

In May 1948, the American Government changed from the election of an American as the Chief Executive Officer. along with members of the U.S House of Representatives and the U.S. Senate, to the candidate (s) by Americans. From said month/year of infamy, no individual may be elected to a national office unless he or she are supported by American Zionist (Jews and Old Testament Christians).

With the death of President Franklin D. Roosevelt, Vice President Harry S. Truman became the President of the United States. Sadly for the American people and the international community, Truman was a Christian Zionist.

May 1948 was also the month an year, Zionist settlers/terrorist announced to the world the occupied land of Palestine was the sovereign country of Israel. Within hours President Truman and Supreme Soviet Leader Joseph Stalin recognized the illegal state of Israel as a nation of the international community.

Truman's recognition of Israel and $400.000 (allegedly 3.1 million today) from Jewish supporters provided the avenue for Truman to win an independent term as President of the United States. To this end, Truman's TREASON through the present day, every American military death in the Middle East, the economic downturn in the United States, and the loss of American respect in the international community began with Truman's Foreign Policy regarding Israel.

The week of April 12 - 16, 2010, the United States is hosting leaders of the international community in Washington, D.C. The gathering is, allegedly, to eliminate additional production by nations currently possessing nuclear weapons and/or increase security among member nations to avoid the possible transfer of nuclear devices to hostile parties.

Iran, North Korea and Syria, the three nations Zionist lie about were not invited to attend. Israel was invited but chose not to attend because, allegedly, their Prime Minister felt the international community would seek clarification to the number of nuclear weapons and delivery systems in the Israeli inventory.

For the record, we learned from historical records that in 1967 two Israeli atomic bombs were armed and 1973 Israel readied 13 atomic bombs destined to destroy targets in Egypt and Syria. More terrifying were the words that Israel would destroy themselves and their enemies rather than surrender.

Recognizing the gravity of the Israeli Atomic Bombs, author Tom Clancy wrote a best seller from which a movie was made. The movie's title was "The Sum of all Fears." (Israeli's lost atomic bomb was recovered, reduced in size, relocated to the United States and concealed in a cigarette machine. Baltimore, MD was destroyed.)

In 1967, Americans serving in the Israeli Defense Forces (IDF) and the IDF launched an air and sea assault against the United States Ship Liberty. (The ship was in international waters monitoring Israel's attack on neighboring Arab nations.) The 1973 use of atomic bombs were the probable option until President Richard M. Nixon authorized the depletion of U.S. Weapons stores to provide Israel with military inventory to defeat the Arabs.

One should note, the depletion of U.S. Military Stores were a Clear and Present Danger to the United States and the North Atlantic Treaty Organization States. (The stores held military resources for joint use by the United States and NATO should the Soviet Union attack a U.S. Ally in Europe or the United States herself.)

President Jimmy Carter's actions with Egypt and Israel cost you and I the American taxpayer billions of dollars prior to the signing of the Camp David Accord and billions each year thereafter. More than two hundred American military personnel were killed in an aircraft crash at Gander, CANADA. The troops were return from a tour in the Sinai Desert per the Camp David Accords.

President Carter was not re-elected because American Zionist and the Israeli Government felt Carter would force more action by the Israeli's to establish a Palestinian nation.

The election of Ronald Reagan, by the Christian Majority and Jewish votes, was responsible for the two hundred plus Marines killed in Lebanon in support occupying Israeli Forces. Worse yet, Reagan authorized hundreds of millions of dollars, if not more, for Israel to build the Lavi Fighter Aircraft for export. (Reagan cared more for the Israelis economy than the American aircraft companies in California and Missouri.)

President George Herbert Walker Bush was handed the results of Reagan's support of Saddam Hussein's war against Iran. The end results of Reagan failed foreign policy was the Persian Gulf War. Bush lost re-election because he and Secretary of State James Baker disapproved of guaranteed loans so Israel could build more illegal structures on the West Bank and other occupied Palestinian land.

President William Jefferson Clinton the 1998 Iraq Liberation Act which charged the government of the United States to remove the elected leader of Iraq, President Saddam Hussein. Clinton didn't order the invasion but authorized a short Iraqi bombing period. (Clinton was more concerned regarding the fossil fuel reserves in Kosovo to deal with Osama bin Laden or Saddam Hussein. The Balkans War was another corporation request to Congress and the Executive Branch that led to the needless loss of lives and destruction. Also, currently Kentucky is receiving a number of Bosnian refugees from the Balkans.)

President George W. Bush and Vice President Richard Cheney entered the White House and immediately began to devise ways in which to obtain the support of the American people to invade Iraq and Afghanistan. (Neither Iraq or Afghanistan had inflicted military damage to the United States or her overseas resources in a act of aggression against our country.) Of interest, it has been reported through several confirmed sources President Bush related God had told him to remove Saddam Hussein, thus, the invasion of Iraq.

The new President of the United States of America, the Honorable Barack H. Obama, was elected without carrying Kentucky and some other Red States. However, he came to the White House with a Zionist Vice President of the United States, Joseph Biden. The House of Representatives is controlled by Zionist and the U.S. Senate. A case and point of his inability to establish a separate but equal nation of Palestine alongside the state of Israel recently came to head: President Obama had asked Israel not to build more apartments in East Jerusalem. Zionist became upset. Then came a letter from Congress with more than 333 House of Representative members, and 76 U.S. Senator's signatures advising Secretary of State Clinton of their displeasure with the actions of President Obama.

Fast forward back to the Nuclear Security Summit in Washington. Israel is known to have approximately 113 nuclear weapons, nuclear subs capable of launching the missiles, and, as previously stated, with aircraft configured to drop or launch the horrific weapons. Israel is the terrorist threat to the international community, not the Arab nations.

Oh, please do not act surprised when I wrote that Israel was a terrorist nation. Just look at the fabricated Old Testament. For example: (1) Abraham the Hebrew and his clan moved into Canaan in search of food and water for his clan and animals. The his family with possessions moved to Egypt. The back to Canaan. (Abraham's flight may be where the name Wander Jew Plant originated.) (2) We have the mythical Moses telling his sons and followers to go into Canaan (Palestine) and kill all the inhabitants, except for virgins. Of course, after killing the indigenous, the Hebrews occupied the land. The IDF continued the murder and occupation of the same people and land in 1967. However, this time, the incident was not a myth.

Another example, of Hebrew (Jewish) mentality is in pre-World War II Germany. The Jews controlled the German Government, accumulated wealth from the German economy. However, they considered themselves Jews and not German citizens.

Different governments in Germany attempted in a number of ways to entice the Jews to become Germans, not a parasite on the nation. Even the government of Adolph Hitler tried to appease the Jews until Germany's military was being defeated by the allies. The results were the terrible deaths of many Europeans, including those of Judaism.

Someone may say that my words regards those of Judaism is wrong but they would be the one incorrect. What the Jews in Germany did is being repeated in the United States as you read this paper. However, in our country, the same situation is worse and it began in 1948 with Truman's TREASON.

President Thomas Jefferson spoke against alliances and the separation of church and state. All presidents since Eisenhower have denied the wisdom of Jefferson and the other founders which has led our nation to one undeclared war after another. For example, the war in Korea and Vietnam were in support of an alliance. Grenada and Panama were political wars to avoid embarrassment. Iraq and Afghanistan are both a religious Crusade and support of the United States Oil Companies.

With regard to the upcoming war with Iran. The last couple of days, I watched to interviews. One was with the President of France and Ms. Katie Couric. When she asked the French President regarding Israel bombing of Iran. The president said it was would be a drastic move. The second interview was with Iran's Chief Nuclear Weapons advisor and Ms. Couric. Asked the same question, the Iranian replied the Middle East would be one fire.

As a disabled military person, I learned first hand what our government did in Southeast Asia. (The people of Cambodia, Laos, and Vietnam did not care the name of their government. Their desire was for the ability for Life, Liberty and the Pursuit of Happiness.) Those in power in Washington do not care about the number of people, including Americans killed, injured, made homeless and the long term illness arising from our weapons and tactics. Their concern is to appease the American Zionist.

In November 2010, the people can rise up and replace the entire House of Representatives and a number of U.S. Senators. A follow-up election in 2012 could remove the remaining senators not running in 2010. Being an American has few responsibilities other than voting. It is time to return to the U.S. Constitution as the foundation of our nation.

Please remember the United States' Government is a Constitutional Republic, not a Theocracy.

With respect, I remain.

Billy Ray Wilson

CONGRESS, ZIONISTS, AND TREASON

Members of Congress have been meeting with President Obama to find avenues to reduce the nation' debts. To this end, allegedly, all government funded programs are on the table for possible reduction. However, there is one illegal expenditure that will not be addressed and that is the unlimited support, both economically and militarily, for the Socialist Country of Israel.

One would assume, in a Constitutional Republic Government, support for a sovereign, socialist, religious dominated government would not enter into the dialog. However, the majority of the US House of Representatives and US Senate owe their existence in Congress to Zionist money and Old Testament voters bloc.

Concurrently in Congress's pipeline of legislation are Senate Resolution 185 and House Resolution 268 awaiting closure.

On June 29, 2011, the Senate passed their resolution; however, final action of the House's Resolution has not been posted.

The purpose of the resolutions are to impose sanctions against and/or suspend funds to the people of Palestine and their representatives. The reason for the resolutions: Israel and the United States demand the Palestinian Authority recognize Israel as a Jewish State.

For crying out loud, the Palestinian Authority and the Arab League have long recognized Israel as the homeland for those of Judaism and the indigenous Israeli Arabs. There can be no recognition of Israel as a Jewish state.

The why is simple, in my opinion, because identifying Israel as a Jewish state would imply there is an existing superior entity that control world events and that God is the God of Abraham. Please, wake up!

Judaism, after all, is but one of three religions fabricated to make the Hebrew Arabs, Christians, and Muslims appear to be superior to the different ethnic tribesman in the land called Palestine and Arabia.

And, with the formation of the religions, a paid clergy and individuals claiming divinity, saw the opportunity to receive money without labor and rule over individuals with an inferiority complex.

The Holy Roman Emperor used Christianity to bring discipline and order to his vast empire. The Prophet Mohammed used his followers to conquer much of the known world and convert the conquered to Islam. A Pope was responsible for the dispatch of armies to liberate Jerusalem. President George W. Bush ordered the last Religious Crusade to remove the President of Iraq and bring Iraq's oil reserves under western control.

Returning to the recognition of Palestinian as a Sovereign nation, the hypocrisy of our country's foreign policy is disgusting. For example, the United Nations, with the consent of the United States Government, recognized the southern region of Sudan, Africa as a sovereign nation. Palestine which has existed for centuries as a land mass, can not be recognized as a sovereign nation.

The difference between southern Sudan and Palestine isn't great. American Christians and international oil companies sought the division of Sudan because southern Sudan has a large Christian population and known oil reserves. Sudan is primarily Muslim dominated. Meanwhile, Palestine is occupied by Israel who seeks the entire land of Palestine as a greater Israel. Oh, allegedly, Gaza has oil reserves which the Israeli want for themselves.

Nothing has changed in the world; Money Lenders are the world's terrorist. In our country, the United States of America, the money lenders have made coup attempts the government of the United States and have kept our country at war. Members of Congress are supposed to be Americans that have the power to terminate the Federal Reserve System and regulate banking commerce. However, our Congress since the 1960s, Americans have not been in the majority. The dual citizenship and Zionist politicians control our government.

Americans, please contact your member of US Congress and ask them to support Palestinian Statehood.

UNSCRUPULOUS FEDERAL GOVERNMENT EMPLOYEES INSTIGATE LIES TO MAKE WAR AND/ OR DEFRAUD THE AMERICAN TAXPAYERS

Having served under the Federal Government's employment umbrella for several decades my highest level of employment was an attachment to a U.S. Embassy Air Attache Office during our country's illegal war in former French Indo-China.

My US Air Force highest position was at Headquarters 22nd Air Force Current Operations Division.

Government contract employment in the Kingdom of Saudi Arabia was as Northup's Aircraft Services Division as Northup's F-5 Squadron Supervisor. A follow-up assignment in the kingdom but with McDonnell Douglas Aircraft Services was as an Administrative Assistant - Operations. with the highest level of employment was my attachment to a U.S. Embassy Air Attache Office.

After departing Department of Defense employment, I advanced to the position of Administrative Officer of the

Day (GS-9), at the VA Medical Center, Louisville, KY.

Yes, I realize I identified my employment history in the Background Chapter; however, herein, I will attempt to show cause for this chapter's title.

Duty at the Air Attache Command & Control Center, provided one with access to the activities of the Defense Intelligence Agency, Central Intelligence Agency, USAID, Air America, Continental Air Services, Bird & Sons, 7/13 Air Force Headquarters, and 7th Air Force Command & Control Center. Also, we worked with indigenous air force personnel in a training mode.

From the cited access, we saw the talent of the employees to make a lie in to the unquestionable truth. We saw embassy officials attempt to deny death benefits to a pilot killed while on a training flight. (A senior US State Department official, in Washington, disagreed with the embassy's message.)

We were part of an operation where a senior government official was, in my opinion, responsible for the needless deaths, injuries, and capture of hundreds of the region's indigenous forces. Lives meant nothing to the American Mission.

And, it is my opinion, our country had a numbered year

plan to be in Southeast Asia and when the pre-established date arrived, the U.S. State Department plan was implemented and we withdrew.

In conjunction with the Indo-China assignment, I was assigned to the Joint Casualty Resolution Center (JCRC). Our mission was to go into Cambodia, Laos, and Vietnam to recover the remains of the US Missing In Action and/or resolve their status via administrative means.

The command's mission, in my opinion, then was not the same as the succeeding command, now stationed in Hawaii, that are recovering remains the former French Indo-China countries.

One such, alleged, MIA remains recovery mission to South Vietnam resulted in the death of an Army Captain and the wounding of his support team. The debrief of the recovery team, to the member, felt the failed mission was just a briefing tool for the departing JCRC General to the Pentagon staff.

Moreover, JCRC personnel expended a great deal of time and effort in providing visiting MIA wives with demonstrations of the expertise of Special Forces, Emergency Disposal Technicians, and others assigned to the recovery team.

Regarding the recovery of administrative (classified) records for MIA Resolution, I was sent on temporary duty to the US Embassy, Vientiane, Laos, to review documents held by the embassy. A side bar was to find 13teen Top Secret documents misplaced by JCRC.

I recovered a large white canvas bag of documents of which pertained to two Air America aircrew members shot down in Laos. Their bodies had been recovered, identified and were awaiting their spouses or next of kin to sign for the remains. I informed my supervisor and so forth. Finally, I had to visit the Deputy Commander of JCRC for assistance in notifying the next of kin who happened to be in Laos seeking permission from the Communist leaders to visit their husband's crash site.

JCRC staff informed the Colonel and me, it wasn't command's responsibility to notify the next of kin. I, in turn, contacted the daughter of an Air America pilot killed in Laos. She, in-turn, notified the wives that their husband's remains were available to be buried.

We, JCRC, were able through aircraft part numbers and other information received from crash sites recommend the change in status from MIA to KIA for a number of the missing Americans. Records reveal the truth on every MIA from the French Indo-China war.

At 22nd Air Force, we saw the misuse of US Air Force resources by politicians and senior military officials. For example, command was ordered to transport the brother of the US President to a foreign capital for non-government business. There is wide misconduct in the armed forces; however, most times, the abuse is created by political pressure.

After 22nd Air Force, I retired and employed by Northup for duty in Saudi Arabia. At the base of employment, we learned US Cargo aircraft would arrive at the air base, their cargo off-loaded, and, in-turn, the cargo would be transferred and on-loaded to one of the many Iraqi aircraft parked on an apron out of eyesight. The following morning, the Iraqi's would file and then depart for Iraq.

More upsetting, in 1989, a group of visiting Pentagon staff officers came to the Saudi Air Base I was employed. We learned the group was visiting each Saudi Air Base, where US Air Force contract overseers and former enlisted personnel versed in Squadron Flight Operations, to ascertain the feasibility of transferring US combat aircraft to the base.

There were no Saudi air force personnel at the squadron on the day of the visit; however, I was in the squadron and provided the group with a tour of the squadron building. A Colonel remarked, the Commander's Office was larger than his office in the Pentagon.

Without a doubt, the purpose of the visit was to identify air bases to support our country's war with Iraq. Based on the visit and the change in the employment environment, especially McDonnell Douglas's staff, I resigned.

On June 18, 2011, while reviewing OpEdNews.com, I came across a news release by Mr. Peter Dale Scott, the title "The Rape in Libya" story - Our military's Latest Fairytale, his story reaffirmed by findings from other documents.

With regards to the Rapes by the Libyan military, where have the American news media and pundits been? It's not right but Africans, as well as other clan/religion dominated societies, have been raping and murdering each other since time began.

More informative too me, in the story, was the following:

-       "When in 1990 Defense Secret Colin Powell was expressing doubts that the United States should attack Kuwait, stories appeared that, as revealed by classified satellite photos, Saddam had amassed 265,000 troops and 1,500 tanks at the edge of the

Saudi Arabian border. Powell then changed his mind. After the invasion, a reporter for the St. Petersburg Times viewed satellite photos from a commercial satellite, and "she saw no sign of a quarter of a million troops or their tanks.""

Worse yet, the stories of the Iraqi military snatching babies from incubators were untrue. The alleged witness had been prepped on her story by the publication relations firm of Hill & Knowlton. The p.r. firm had a 11.5 million dollar contract with the Kuwaiti government.

The story went on to say that hawks in Congress such as the late Congressman Tom Lantos and Congressman Stephen Solarz secured support for the attack on Iraq using the Kuwaiti incubator story. (Tom Lantos was a Jew and Israeli first. He and his fellow Zionist are responsible for an unknown number of dead Americans and billions of dollars expended for Zionist causes. He was a TRAITOR.)

As previously written in this book, Congress is responsible for the current wars hostile environments in Afghanistan and Iraq. Also, without a doubt, a powerful committee chairmen in both the House and Senate, are behind the so-called Arab Spring. However, I read where one country's citizens were calling to end the monarchy.

Their citizens may want to stay their action for a period and, look instead, to the United States of America. Our founders worried about the loss of our Republic is valid as today, no American can be elected to a national official without they cower to the Zionist of the United States. The worries materialized, the United States is no longer a Republic but a corporate theocracy.

Regarding employment at the Department of Veterans Affairs. I arrived at the Louisville VA Medical Center to a GS-3 position following a transfer from the Allen Park, MI VA Medical Center. I rose through the ranks to position of Administrative Officer of the Day.

In this position, I was responsible, after normal duty hours, for the administrative actions of the Admissions Section and assisting the Emergency Room with the completion of Lab Test Forms and X-Ray request plus whatever administrative needs arose.

At admissions, we processed new arrivals at the medical center seeking health care benefits from the Department of Veterans. To this end arose my major fault with the Department of Veterans.

With the election of President William Jefferson Clinton and First Lady Hillary Clinton, the VA became involved in the President and First Lady's Health Care scheme for the nation.

The administration change to allow Non-Service Connected Veterans to receive the same benefits as Service Connected Veterans made me uneasy. (Even with my doubts, I completed every transaction with the new arrival as prescribed by VA policy and regulation.) The individual was not required to have shed blood on the battlefield or bore the battle. The prerequisite was a Honorable or Under Honorable Condition Discharge.

The new policy charged the NSC person with obtaining a clinic and doctor; whereas, he or she could receive medical care and medications at any VA Medical Center or Clinic.

As a health care patient, the NSC person could receive his or her medication at the price charged to Service Connected (SC) Veterans. In this light, the former military person may have a monthly medication bill for each prescription costing in the hundreds or more. However, as a VA patient, he or she could purchase their medications at the rate of $2.00 (1998 prices) per prescription.

Moreover, it the veteran fell below the poverty line, he or she were eligible for a NSC pension. If married his spouse could be enrolled in the CHAMP VA Program.

She too would receive care at the expense of the American taxpayer. These individuals most likely are listed as Priority 7 or 8 for health care.

The only negative element to the NSC care, if any, was if the NSC person had the money to pay for care, he or she was charged a co-pay.

Recently, Congressman Ryan is seeking legislation to remove the Priority 7 and 8 NSC veterans from receiving aid from the Department of Veterans Affairs.

President Abraham Lincoln and President Theodore Roosevelt sought health care and benefits for the veteran that shed his blood and bore the battle. If deceased, the veteran's widow and children would be cared for by a grateful nation. Soliciting votes demeaned, in my opinion, the U.S. Military Veteran.

Returning to the subject title story, the following is a quote of the last four sentence of his story: "It is painful to say this, but virtually every major U.S. military intervention since Korea has been accompanied by false stories. Mr. Moreno-Ocampo should be pressed to come forward quickly with the supporting evidence for his charges, which should be based on more than the testimony of doctors working for the Benghazi regime."

Sadly, human beings have been led to believe in untruths since the beginning of time. The greatest lie of all is the God of Abraham. (Get a DNA test, learn your true forefathers. End the lie, save our Republic.)

CONGRESSIONAL FAILURE TO ASSURE AIR SAFETY, STANDARDIZED POLICIES, AND EQUALITY FOR THE DISABLED

DENIED PASSAGE

The Congress of the United States of America is a most powerful entity in our country of which members are, through the dictates of the U.S. Constitution, charged to defend the U.S. Constitution against all enemies both foreign and domestic. They are the representatives of the people; whereas, they have oversight over the presidential administration in power, allocate funds, approve/disapprove treaties, etc. In essence, they are the powers that assure the prosperity and security of the United States.

And, since Congress changed, with the 20th Amendment of the U.S. Constitution, their call to session from the 1st Monday in December to noon, January 3, Congressional members have gone from citizen/legislator to legislator as a vocation.

The 20th Amendment has allowed members of Congress to remain in Washington in an continuous oversight position instead of meeting once a year and/or at such time recalled to Washington by the President for an emergency session.

As a retired military Master Sergeant with 35 years employment experience which the majority was under the federal governments umbrella, I find the change worrisome.

The why is that with Congress being in Washington as legislators instead of citizen/legislators, human nature tells one, human beings become corrupted and interference with the Constitutional duties of the President of the United States.

The corruption by Congress has changed Congress from being manned by Americans to individuals with dual citizenship and loyalty to their religion. Per the Declaration of Independence and the U.S. Constitution, all Americans are equal and this nation is a Constitutional Republic, not a theocracy.

Worse yet, if that's possible, members of Congress are producing legislation that funds and charges the President to commit acts of war against nations of the international community. For example, previously identified, the 1998 Iraq Resolution Act sent the nation to war.

On a human basis, members of Congress go to Washington, in most part, as poor or middle class Americans; however, by the end of their tenures in Washington, these individuals have cumulated wealth.

Yes, the wealthy become richer.

From the oversight positions I addressed, members of Congress through enacted laws provide large corporations and friends of Congress, legislation that allows them to defraud the American people and keep our military forces in a state of war.

A personal example was a February 2011 flight to Bangkok, Thailand. In this light, I have provided copies of documentation I wrote to the Bangkok Nation, United Airlines and Delta Airlines. My health and life were endangered by the policies of the airlines which, allegedly, were approved by the Congressional Oversight of the Airlines.

A day or so past, ABC Evening News reported that Delta Airlines charged returning U.S. military personnel for checked baggage. The military's uproar was heard, mine was not.

As our fellow Americans know, members of Congress do not have the problems encountered by the average

American. The ride at taxpayers expense or gratis aboard corporate aircraft while some ride in style on U.S. Special Mission Aircraft.

I realize I am but one person and I realize also that I am not the disabled or non-disabled American that encountered the arrogance of the airlines.

We need to end the employment of members of Congress as full time legislators. We need to return to the citizen/legislator. With the electronic and data system so readily available, there is not need for a member of Congress year around in Washington.

FEDERAL RESERVE AND CORRUPT MEMBERS OF CONGRESS

Once again, a political party in the Congress of the United States of America is about to close down our government. To further my knowledge of our country's financial history, I began researching for this Letter to the Editor and OpEdNews.com. My sources were the Internet Web Sites and earlier prints of the World Book Encyclopedia.

Per my research, the following three quotes by two family members, among the group of individuals, that control the Federal Reserve Banking System of the United States:

Mayer Amschel Rothschild (23 February 1744 - 19 September 1812): Born in "Judengasse" or Jew Alley, Frankfurt am Main, Germany. He was the founder of the Rothschild family international banking dynasty. His nationality was German.

Mr. Mayer Amschel Rothschild's quote on banking; "Let me issue and control a nation's money and I care not who writes the laws."

In 1798, Mr. Rothschild's third son, Nathan Mayer Rothschild was sent to England to open the family's first foreign bank. He took with him 20,000 million pounds capital to further the family's interest in textiles.

Nathan Rothschild (1777-1836): "I care not what puppet is placed on the throne of England to rule the empire. The man who control Britain's money supply control the British Empire and I control the British money supply."

Mayer A. Rothschild's two older sons were sent to other European cities to accumulate more wealth throughout whatever means. For example, the Rothschild's Gold was used to finance Britain's many aggressive adventures throughout the world. Another usage, by the Rothschilds, was to pay German Hessians to create turmoil in the American colonies.

An American member of the Federal Reserve Board is David Rockefeller. Mr. Rockefeller is the youngest and only surviving son of John D. Rockefeller. He turned down being the Chairman of the Federal Reserve Board but nominated Paul Volker.

His father, John D. Rockefeller, was present at the meeting in 1913 to establish another privately owned banking system in the United States along with representatives for the Rothschilds plus a relative of the Bush family. The new banking entity was named the Federal Reserve Bank.

There was some controversy regarding Mr.David Rockefeller's stand on the establishment of a One World Order. He responded to a challenger: "If that the charge I stand guilty, and I'm proud of it."

From reading the biography of David Rockefeller, I do not believe he would do anything, unlike the Rothschilds, to harm the United States of America. (Recommend Americans read the history of this remarkable American.)

Digressing to the financial times in the American colonies, I must first report the views of a few of our founders and Chief Executives opinion of individuals who sought to render the financial affairs of the United States to a Rothschild or like banking system:

George Washington called the "our greatest enemy." Benjamin Franklin "Vampires" and "Asiatic" (a race of Khazars from Asia.). Thomas Jefferson "false citizens." Andrew Jackson "ye, breed of vipers."

Former President James Madison was blunt: "money changers have used every form abuse, intrigue, deceit, and violet means possible to maintain their control over governments by controlling money and its issuance."

Benjamin Franklin said the American Revolution was not about taxes but money. "We issue our own money called Colonial Scrip. In creating our own paper money, we control its purchasing power and have not interest to pay one."

Franklins words were heard during a visit to England, in turn, the British Government ordered the colonies to cease and detest in issuing their own currency.

Several American Presidents sought to void our country's reliance upon the Rothschilds Banking System. However, there were short periods of non-reliance. For example, during such a period, President Andrew Jackson paid off our national debt. The only American President to do so.

Sadly, the Rothschilds and old money families assumed control of the Federal Reserve in 1913. To this end, in my opinion, the only way non-government entities could assume the mantle of financial control over the United States is through TREASON by American politicians. For example, at the 1913 meeting besides the bankers and their representatives were Theodore Roosevelt and Woodrow Wilson. (My research did not reveal whether Roosevelt or Wilson agreed to the establishment of the non-federal banking entity.)

For myself, I have witnessed possible government shutdown previously in my lifetime and, I know without a doubt, the United States, through the Department of Treasury, has the ability to administer the fiscal needs of the United States without private bankers.

Benjamin Franklin's Colonial Scrip added to the prosperity of the colonies. I used Military Scrip when I was in Korea during the early 1960s. Each state could issue their own monetary units while the federal government takes in taxes to accomplish the tasking of the United States Constitution. Allow the states to administer their states without federal interference.

With regards to the banking industry that put our country in this mess, I do not know why the federal government needed to bail out the banks of New York City. Without a doubt, should a honest committee investigate the questionable banks transactions, they would find the banks knowingly knew their loans were a risky but, also knew, members of Congress and the Presidential Administration would bail them out

Proof of our government protecting bankers and investors all one needs to do is to investigate the reasons we invaded Afghanistan. The Afghanistan government or the people of

Afghanistan did nothing harmful against the United States. However, for more than one Presidential Administration and the tenures of a number of members of Congress, our government supported building oil and gas pipelines through Afghanistan to Pakistan and, eventually, India. One deal alone will cost investors more than 7 billion dollars.

Construction contracts let in Afghanistan will not be completed until the year 2014; therefore, members of the US Congress who are demanding a demand a life time occupation of Afghanistan will achieve their quest by killing and maiming Americans for fossil fuel and vast mineral deposits waiting to be mined.

Oh, one must not forget, our presence in Afghanistan is as Afghanistan borders Iran which is a future target for the money changers and the members of the US Congress.

By the way, Iraq was a selected target for invasion at least a decade before the actual invasion. The oil corporations and Israel could not allow Saddam Hussein to control the vast oil resources needed by the West.

Moreover, Zionist, AIPAC, the government of Israel could not stand idly by and watch the Iraq military and government reach a point to where the Iraq's attained the same great power as the leaders of ancient Babylon.

And, for those that don't remember their history, the ancient people of present day Iraq, conquered and enslaved some Hebrew Arabs, while other Hebrew Arabs remained in Babylon as it was after all, " the Cradle of Civilization."

In Babylon, Hammurabi, one of the greatest kings of Babylonia, were the first laws for civilized man - the Code of Hammurabi. No longer could a village elder or wealth land owner deny a citizen of what was hers or his.

Of course, the Hebrew Arabs , whether they were in Babylon by choice or not, had the opportunity to visit Babylon's Library and other centers of learning. From this opportunity came the writings of Hebrew scribes who turned the existing laws, life without suffering from thirst or starvation and tranquil life from the Babylonians to the Hebrew Arabs.

A case in point is currently in review by the US State Department and the Iraqi Government involves Hebrew Arab books and other materials rescued from a sewage filled Baghdad basement during the 2003 invasion.

Moreover, during an interview following the fall of Baghdad, a citizen of Baghdad responded to a news reporter that his religion was Judaism but he was an Iraqi. Another replied, an independent oil pipeline was operational between Iraq and Israel.

An alert reader may ask "What does the Hebrew Arabs and Israel have to do with the Federal Reserve and Corrupt Members of Congress?" The answer is money.

As I wrote at the beginning, the President and members of Congress are meeting to discuss a financial bailout for the United States. Allegedly, words from the White House and Congress are that all expenditures by the federal government will be on the table for possible deduction. However, the economic and military support for the Socialist country of Israel will not be addressed.

One would assume, in a Constitutional Republic Government, support for a sovereign, socialist, religious dominated government, Israel, would not be a topic of discussion. However, the majority of the members of the US House of Representatives and the US Senate could not have been elected without Zionist money and Old Testament voter's bloc.

Another hot subject in the Middle East is the recognition of Palestine as a sovereign nation on-going since 1947. Sadly, there are two resolutions, 185 & 268, pending in Congress. The Senate has approved their resolution.

The purpose of the resolutions are to impose sanctions against and/or suspend funds to the people of Palestine and their representatives if they go ahead an seek state hood recognition at the United Nations September 2011. The US and Israel are demanding the Palestinian Authority recognize Israel as a Jewish State.

But, wait, the Palestinian Authority and the Arab League for decades have recognized Israel as a homeland for Jews (Hebrew Arabs) and the indigenous Israeli Arabs. There can be no recognition of Israel as a Jewish state.

The why Israel is not a Jewish State, in my opinion, is because acknowledgement would imply there is an existing superior entity that control world events and that God and/or superior being is the God of Abraham.

Judaism, religion of Jews, is but one of three religions fabricated to make the Hebrew Arabs, Christians, and Muslims, respectively, appear superior to the different ethnic tribesman in the land called Palestine and Arabia.

And, even though Judaism originated with a fabricated God, the God and his followers opened the avenue for power and wealth. However, over the centuries, the reported richest men on earth's religion has been/is Judaism.

Some may say that religion affiliation does not matter in the scheme of life. However, you and I both know, the belief is untrue. For example, let us remind everyone that it was the Rothschilds, a former Chief Justice of the US Supreme Court, Mr. Eddie Jacobson, boyhood friend and partner of the American traitor, Harry S. Truman, responsible for Israel's statehood on the diplomatic front. (You don't want to forget the Supreme Soviet Leader Joseph Stalin, he followed Truman in recognizing Israel.)

I've strayed a bit regarding statehood for a new nation. Although, our members of Congress will not accept Palestine, our government recently recognized Southern Sudan as an independent nation. One may wonder if the fact the south had oil reserves and many of the population were Christians.

Oh, many may not be familiar but the Gaza part of the occupied land of the Palestinians is known to have oil and gas reserves. The Israeli want the fossil fuels. I suppose religion and oil does mix.

Digress back in years for a moment. One may remember the

hostile action in the Serbia and Kosovo during the Clinton Administration. Well, Kosovo is now an independent country with oil reserves.

As a disabled American Military veteran of the former French Indo-China nations war, the Federal Reserve and members of the US Congress are killing and maiming Americans, plus citizens of the countries, we invade or demean on a daily basis for oil and religion. Surely, Americans will rise up and return our government to the people.

MILITARY MEMBER SATURATE THE POLLS IN 2012 & 2014!!!!

Allegedly, June 4, 2011, was the largest deployment of Kentucky's National Guard since World War II. On this date, Kentucky's 1149th Forward Support Company deployed to Iraq. Their tasking, base defense and logistical support for U.S. Armed Forces occupying Iraq.

As a disabled, military retiree, but most of all an American, it is time for U.S. military active duty, military reserves, national guardsmen, Coast Guard, and military retirees to make arrangements to vote either by absentee ballot or at the polling stations.

Yes, the 2012 and 2014 national elections are a long way off; however, the importance of these elections demand your efforts to assure Americans are the helm of power in our national capital.

Today, we have Congressional members and a Vice President, Joseph Biden, that have dual citizenship and/or declared Zionist. These individuals commit TREASON in the name of a fabricated God and for U.S./British/French Oil Companies to own and/or control the international supply of fossil fuels.

Yes, the 1st Amendment of the U.S. Constitution guarantees freedom of religion; however, our country is a

Constitutional Republic. Regardless of what the clergy, religious zealots and the media pundits declare, the United States is not now nor ever a Christian nation and/or, like Zionist believe, a Judeo-Christian Nation.

Yes, from personal experience, the all volunteer military became an avenue for Americans to achieve their goals. Some military personnel performed their tasks as a regular employment position while wearing a uniform; an opportunity to receive a college education; for me, an chance to receive an education, be employed, travel the world, and get away from religious brainwashing. Others, more dedicated members which included me, gave their all everyday.

Yes, without a doubt, there are those in the military that enjoy killing and destruction but they, I believe, are a miniority. Also, there are individuals in order to receive medals/awards and promotions, they become like those Americans in Congress, Presidential Cabinet, and appointed positions within the government. They are without morals.

Moreover, regardless of the incentives to enlist, each and every military member swore to defend the U.S. Constitution against all enemies foreign and domestic and obey the orders of those appointed by Congress to lead the military. However, the Uniform Code of Military

Justice stipulates, a military member may disobey an order, he or she deems unlawful. (Of course, he or she will suffer for a period until such time a Court has delivered the verdict. If the member was correct, your decision will stand. Hard choice but the only one for an American military member.)

Of note, it is my wish the Department of Defense would include in the oath of enlistment, words and spirit of the Declaration of Independence. Such a decision could assist in eliminating the practice of calling oneself by their ancestry and/or their religion. There are no hyphenated Americans in the U.S. Military. We are all Americans and/or in the process of becoming an American.

What is the definition of domestic and foreign enemies, in my opinion?

Are domestic enemies foreign sleeper agents, worshipers of a non-Judeo-Christian God, individuals residing in the United States as non-Americans, citizens that identify themselves by their ancestry/ethnic group rather than citizens of the United States, and/or members of the Legislative and Executive Branches of the United States Government?

Are foreign enemies, the governments of nations and/or

groups within those nations that do not prescribe to U.S./Zionist Foreign Policy? Of the twenty countries, I visited either by duty or travel, I never heard anyone demean the United States because of our rights under the U.S. Constitution that assures prosperity and security.

Yes, I did hear some Saudi military personnel that had trained in the United States speak of the clubs and women of the night. To their remarks, I responded, drink and prostitution came to Arabia long before the United States and both still exist in the kingdom. (Money buys anything.)

With regards to domestic enemies, it is my opinion, the religious community and national leaders elected with Jewish and Zionist Christians' monetary contributions and religious oriented voting blocks are the enemies of the American people.

Moreover, the most recent example of religious domination presented its ugly self following a Middle East Peace Message by President Obama. Immediately, Zionist within the United States population declared the President "Threw Israel Under The Bus" and multiple equally appalling statements. Our country is the United States of America, not the Socialist Country of Israel.

As to foreign enemies, there isn't a nation on the planet Earth that poses a danger to the United States. In fact, our alleged foreign enemies are identified as such because, their governments or groups within the country allegedly pose a threat to the state of Israel.

The cause of the discourse between the alleged terrorist within the United States and the international community of Islam, came in to being in May 1948. This was the date, when President Harry S. Truman recognized the occupation of Palestine by Zionist terrorist as a sovereign nation of Israel. Since said date, the international community has known nothing but turmoil.

Hopefully, what I wrote about Israel and the religious community did not offend as it was not my intent. American military members are citizens from all over the United States and territories. We are not in battle or hostilities like the Religious Crusades of centuries past, we are supposed to defend the U.S. Constitution against all enemies foreign and domestic. No religious leader sends Americans to fight. Congress declares war and provides money for the war, not Rome, Mecca, or Jerusalem.

My countrymen, it is time for the military's leadership to stand up and say no to future hostilities. Unless Congress declares war or a foreign army strikes the states of the United States or territories, the saber stays in the scabbard.

GUIDANCE TO ACTIVE DUTY AND RETIRED MEMBERS OF THE UNITED STATES ARMED FORCES

Congress will kill you and deny payment of benefits

The title may sound odd from a retired, disabled Air Force Master Sergeant, former Department of the Army Civilian and former Department of Veterans Affairs medically retired GS-9.

During my career in the U.S. Air Force, my body was subject to many, many different types of immunizations. The immunizations enabled us to deploy to any country around the world while knowing we were immunized for the most common diseases of that region and/or Anthrax.

And, to the air force's credit, the living quarters, dinning facilities, off-duty recreations and medical clinics were built with the needs of the airman in mind. However, at special assignments. one lived off the economy, wore civilian attire and bonded with the indigenous. The living standards and environment in ever aspect was different from the United States.

On a typical day, you may have to wade a rice patty to string wire or other tasks that have a tendency to pop up away from a fixed airbase, garrison, or camp. The air you breath may be filled with metallic dust or other than the air of the United States. The water is not potable; whereas, you assume the third country nationals charged to purify the water did their jobs. The fruits and vegetables may have arrived from areas just sprayed by Agent Orange or some other toxic fluid. The local government with the assistance of the US AID mission and/or contractor sprays to kill the insects leaving a cloud of black, smelly smoke. A contractor is called to rid your neighborhood of Cobra snakes, camel or banana spiders, scorpions, and natures other killers of people.

The indigenous you teach, respect very few safety practices, ask assistance to move barrels and other containers with you not knowing the contents. The building you work in, you have no ideal on what toxic dump the structure was built.

Driving on the highways or riding local buses or contracted buses for transport to and from your duty station is somewhat dangerous due to the driver's lack of adherence to post laws and signals.

A mile or so from your quarters is a company or more of Communist forces that would like nothing better than to kill you.

If deployed to forward operating locations, one is not sure if your covert headquarters will dispatch airlift to return you to your point of residence. Even worse, should you be stranded at a site deep within Communist held territory, will the command provide night air support to keep you safe.

The food you eat in the local restaurants or that cooked by your maid, you are not sure the origin of the food stuff. The ice you put in your drinks, may be made of un-potable water. The sodas or alcohol drinks may be regionally made other than the US brands you thought you purchased.

If you get injured in the field, too often, you are told to shake it off and continue. Then when later in your life, the injured area matures or becomes inflamed, there is no medical record of you injury.

Your work site may contain Weapons of Mass Destruction which were sealed at their point of origin; however, a number of people without proper training have handled the devices which could have resulted in a seal broken or a leak.

Worse yet, working and transiting areas that were struck with Uranium tipped weapons, gasses employed prior to your arrival, and/or exposure to the many new weapons both the US and enemy forces introduced in every theatre of fighting.

After your deployment or assignment is over and you return to the United States, your health begins to deteriorate immediately or it may take 40 -50 years to mature. You go to a military doctor or, if retired, you go to the nearest Veterans Administration (VA) Hospital.

For the VA hospital, you enter the building and are directed to proceed to the admissions section. The person at the desk will ask you so many questions that you may become angry. You ask yourself why aren't they concerned about my health and questions pertaining to income, if your have Medicare, Medicaid, or any other type of insurance.

Finally, after a long period of time waiting in the Emergency Room, first time applicants, your are seen by a Triage Nurse. Eventually, you will see a doctor, practicing nurse or Patient Assistant (PA).

Finally, you have been seen, your aliment diagnosed and medication is prescribed. Sometime later or maybe after completing the applicable for medical benefits, your were told that since your were not service connected for the ailment, then you may have to pay for the hospital visit.

Of note, I recall one evening on duty as an Administrative Officer of the Day, at the Louisville VA Medical Center, a retired military member that had served in World War II, Korea and Vietnam arrived for emergency care. To date, he had not applied for any service connected medical problems. The retiree was charged for his visit.

Payment for hospital care, if not service connected, is based on your income and ability to pay for health care.

The ideal of providing gratis health care and support for widows and orphans originated with President Abraham Lincoln and followed up by President Theodore Roosevelt. Their criteria was that veteran must have borne the battle and shed his blood.

Enter President William Jefferson Clinton and his First Lady, Madam Hillary Rodham Clinton. With the First Lady deeply involved in a national health care system, soon the gates were open for hospital care for the Non-Service Connected (NSC) and, of course the Service Connected (SC) veteran. The NSC and SC veterans could apply at their hospital and if assigned a clinic and doctor, they would be able to purchase medication at the Department of Veterans rate; however for the NSC person, if above the poverty level, he or she was charged for their visit and medication. The SC veteran below a specified disabled rating had to pay for their medications and visit, if the aliment wasn't SC. Above the established health care, including optical, dental, were gratis plus the veteran received disability complementation based on their disability rating, dependents, etc.

With the Clinton's new program, the hospital began registering individuals that may or may not have completed basic training or their contracted years and, more importantly in my eyes, never departed the Continental United States for a hostile environment. Their only prerequisite for care and compensation was they received a Honorable or Under Honorable Condition Discharge.

But, the kicker and my opinion may be wrong, if the NSC person fell below the poverty line, then he or she received their health care, including dental, optical, etc, gratis plus a NSC pension.

Being from southeastern Kentucky, I was upset that individuals could receive the benefits identified because following their short military service, he or she did not pay in to Social Security or monetarily provide for their retirement. They became, in essence, a ward of both the state and federal government.

Please do not misunderstand what I wrote regarding the NSC veteran. Sure, there were individuals who enlisted, at the encouragement of Armed Forces Recruiters, who were not mentally or physically qualified for military duty.

Yes, it is a fact that some recruiters tell their applicants not to report medications taken or other medical related problem that could derail their enlistment. (I know this happens, I said the results of unethical military recruiters during my employment at the Louisville VA Medical Center. Yes, I reported the practice.)

The new enlistee would go to Fort Knox for example, begin his or her military training and within a short time they would be admitted to the psych floor of the medical center. The cost to the American taxpayer increased as the individual was discharged; whereas, some government agency will have to assume the cost of his or her maintenance.

What could resolve the problem of recruiting unfit applicant is two fold. The first would be to replace the military recruiters at fault with recruiters that are ethical. The second is that Congress cease and detest in starting illegal wars that create a need for additional military personnel.

Regarding creating wars, June 12, 2011, I read an article by Joshua Holland, AlterNet, regarding military cost. They are follows:

-       "This year, we'll spend $170 billion to keep troops in Iraq and Afghanistan, and I think that's a handy weigh of expressing big numbers. It works out to $465 million each and every day, or $19.4 million per hour."

-       "Republican Paul Ryan and the House of Representatives are looking to end VA healthcare for over 1.3 million veterans who are Priority 7 & 8. These veterans are the least disabled veterans using the system, usually with disability ratings of 0 percent or no service-connected disability. According to the Congressional Budget Office "Option 35," the cuts would leave 130,000 veterans with no healthcare alternative. This means veterans with conditions not recognized by the VA, like certain diseases from Agent Orange exposure, would have to pay for healthcare out of pocket if they had not other service connect disability."

- "Currently, the VA spends over $4 billion yearly to treat these vets, despite co-pays intended to offset the expense. Ryan's cuts are intended to save $6 billion off the VA's tab and $62 billion over the next 10 years. Instead of merely increasing the co-pay or taxing Wall Street, Congress wants to just cut your benefits, all together."

"So the GOP would cut 1.3 million vets off of VA health-care--way to support those troops, fellas!--in order to save the equivalent of what it cost to keep troops in Afghanistan and Iraq for 12.9 days."

Now to my guidance. Each and every time you are injured in any way in the military whether on duty or off duty, report to a medical clinic and make sure a record is made. A person has a hard enough time from the VA's Regional Office in requesting disability based on their military service without a medical record of the injury or incident.

Your commander may send you to a psych doctor because of your doctor or clinic visits but it is your health that must be cared for at your retirement or end of your contracted duty. Take care of yourself.

Equally important to retaining medical records are copies of your administrative for transfers, temporary duty or any other order that affects your career and/or physical profile. Also, each time your read an article regarding the disabilities or sickness caused by duty in foreign countries, be sure to save a copy.

If assigned to a covert assignment, if legal, photograph an object and/or landmark that identifies your presence in-country. Be careful. In Saud Arabia, for instance, all government buildings are considered classified. In Buddhist countries make sure you do not sit on or deface in any way shape or form, a likeness of Buddha. In Thailand never mishandle money in any way. The likeness of the King is imprinted in the money.

And, I am sorry to report that should you be assigned to a covert assignment, either permanent party or temporary duty, should you file a claim for disability with your local Veterans Administration Regional Office, you will be in for a set back. For example, from the Vietnam era, the Department of Veterans Affairs came up with this ruling: You did not have boots on the ground in the Republic of South Vietnam.

In Iraq, Afghanistan, Israel, and the other nations involved in Congress' war on Islam and seizure of oil reserves, there will be other nations, your VA Regional Office want recognize your presence.

Keep abreast of communications from the Department of Veterans Affairs and the Department of Defense. Your physical health and economic survival depend on your personal actions. You can not rely on our government to be truthful or support the veteran.

The boots on the ground logic is a simple way to deny earned compensation. It was the US Government, after all, that ordered your presence in a hostile environment without the knowledge or consent of the Congress of the United States.

Maybe worse than the VA's Regional Office and some VA Medical Centers are the members of Congress that say the US can not afford to pay for the SC Veteran and, now, the NSC Veteran. But, hey, the members of Congress and the President of the United States are the reasons for your disability.

However, since World War II, the Congress of the United States hasn't Declared War. These so-called honorable men and women have allowed a President to deploy the military when the alleged enemy did not physically attack the United States.

Some may question my statement the physical attack on the United States. The country of Afghanistan did not do any harm against the United States or the American people. In fact, the war was initiated by the Congress in their 1998 Iraq Liberation Act. This Act funded and ordered the President to remove Saddam Hussein, Iraq's Head of State. Acts if war, President Clinton signed the act but did not order the invasion of Afghanistan or Iraq.

In 2006, Congress legislated the Iran Freedom and Support Act which was signed by the President. This funded and charged the President with interfering with the government of Iran.

Of note, recently retired US Army General Wesley Clark reported that once while in the Pentagon, he was told there were five nations to be engaged following the Iraq/Afghanistan Conflict.

My fellow Americans make sure you record all harmful activities in your life and, above all, be sure to vote in every election for true Americans. Per the US Constitution dual citizenship Americans are not eligible to hold public office.

The United States of America is the people's country, not Corporations, Wall Street Bankers, and religious zealots You swore an oath to defend the Constitution, then do so..

HOMELESS US VETERANS UNDERSTANDABLE

July 17, 2011, I read a story written by Mr. Sadeq Lavasani, released by PRESS TV and narrated by Sarbas Nazari, Subject: 75,000 US veterans face homelessness. To this end, based upon the interference with the US Constitution, the homeless are understandable.

The reasons for why there will be 75,000 US veterans homelessness on any given night in June 2011 came from the United States Constitution original draft. The drafters of the US Constitution recognized each state's militias, and gave them vital roles to fill: "to execute the Laws of the Union, suppress Insurrections and repel Invasion." (My copy of the Constitution reads: "To provide for calling forth the militia to execute the Laws of the Union, suppress Insurrections and repel invasions.") Congress gave the President power to decide when a state of invasion or insurrection (uprising) exists.

States maintained dominant control over their National Guards until 1916. That year, Congress approved the National Defense Act which provided for federal funding of the guard and for drafting the guard into national service under certain circumstances.

Moreover, the Act established the right of the President to "Federalize" the National Guard, in the time of a declared emergency. Control of the National Guard reverted back to the states once the declared emergency ended.

From the original draft of the US Constitution, the status of state's militias in relationship to the Army of the United Sates has changed a number of times. The following four (4) Congressional changes should be noted:

1. The Total Force Policy, 1973. Requires all active and reserve military organization be treated as a single force.

2. The Montgomery Amendment to the National Defense Act for Fiscal Year 1987: provides that a Governor cannot withhold consent with regard to active duty outside the United States because of nay objection to the location, purpose, or schedule of such duty.

3. The John Warner Defense Authorization Act 2007 Public Law 109-364. Federal law was changed in section 1076 so that the Governor of a state is no longer the sole commander in chief of their state's National Guard during emergencies within the state. The President of the United States will now be able to take total control of a state's National Guard units without the Governor's consent. All 50 Governors opposed the power of the President over the National Guard.

4. The National Defense Authorization Act 2008 Public Law 110-181. Repeals provisions in section 1076 in Public Law 109-364 but still enables the President to call up the National Guard of the United States for active federal military service during Congressionally sanctioned national emergency or war. Places the National Guard Bureau directly under the Department of Defense as a joint activity.

(Note: information regarding the National Guard was retrieved from a Internet Free Information Web Site.)

As a retired Air Force Air Operations Superintendent and former employee at the Veterans Administration Medical Center, prior to being medically retired, the ability of the federal government to activate National Guardsmen and Reservist now makes sense.

From the position of Administrative Officer of the Day, Admissions and Emergency Room Administrative assistance, we learned from Army trainees that certain military recruiters would inform their enlistees not to disclose certain medical information that would deny enlistment. However, once under the guidance, of too often unethical drill instructors, the trainees disabilities would manifest itself. The trainees were cannon fodder for the illegal military adventures created by the Congress of the United States.

Naturally, not all the hospitalized trainees were future National Guard or Reservist. Many were to become "All You Can Be," active duty US Army.

National Guard members were once citizen-soldiers. During their daily lives, they were employed in their hometowns as doctors, lawyers, merchants, drivers, carpenters, etc. However, at certain periods during the year, he or she must attend their National Guard meetings and attend active duty training, when scheduled. Should a state emergency arise, he or she accepted the challenge without question. The member, at one time, knew once the emergency was resolved, they would return to their neighborhood and their families.

However, with Congress making the National Guard and Reserve Forces part of the nation's active duty forces; Guardsmen and Reservist are deployed throughout the international community to engage in armed conflicts without a Declaration of War.

To me the utilization of National Guardsmen and Reservist as part of the Congressional designated Army strength is un-Constitutional. Moreover, to allow the President of the United States to be the Commander In Chief of Guardsmen and Reservist without a Declaration of War returns our nation to the unlimited power of a monarch. (The Declaration of Independence addressed charged against the British Monarch for what now our President has been given by Congress.

And, due to the constant deployments, the non-active duty members, along with active duty forces, are exposed to the unfavorable environments of foreign nations and the indigenous goal of killing their American occupiers. Equally troublesome, the American military members is subjected to the adverse effects of American weaponry such as depleted Uranium. Also, as in the Vietnam era, the service member's lives were further endangered by politicians, US State Department officials and promotion seeking military commanders.

What the members of Congress do not care nor the American people realize that you can not take a young American unaccustomed in killing and maiming another human being and, equally bad, once in country, learn the reasons for their deployment was a lie. However, it is too late for the service member for he or she has killed and/or been instrumental in the deaths of the living and subjected to mental stress never conceived in the United States.

Moreover, the negative elements of the foreign environment and the toxic substances used by our government will mature in a number of years, depending of the toxin, and the true military veteran will no longer have the will to exist in a society that allowed the government to impair or kill them.

Of extreme interest, no foreign government has attacked the United States since Pearl Harbor. All other military actions since 1941 have been for political purposes, assure corporate America foreign resources for their profit, and, as with Iraq, a Religious Crusade.

Yet, the American people, especially the religious community, have become so comfortable with their lives, they care not for the country or the military members they send off to die, maim, or make anti-social.

Billy Ray Wilson
209 Autumn Drive
London, KY 40744-7071
(606) 862-2847

ISRAEL

THE INTERNATIONAL TERRORIST

From childhood forward until I entered the United States Air Force on 30 September 1960, we learned about the Hebrew Arabs, the prophets, Moses, Noah, Jesus Christ, the Romans and the first civilized city/state - Babylon.

The Hebrew Arabs were always in some type of hostilities or dispute with the regions powers. Never mentioned was the fact that the Hebrew Arabs were of the same race and were contributing partners in their communities. Abraham, later known in the religious community as Abraham the Hebrew as, allegedly, a wealthy Arab, with a large clan with multiple wives. His township at the beginning was Ur, present day Iraq.

We learned from religious writings that Abraham and his clan was forced to move to Canaan (Palestine) because of a drought in Ur. He and his clan moved about like the parasite plant, the Wandering Jew. No land space existed that Abraham's clan would not enter to provide foodstuff and water for the live stock and family members.

We were taught that Moses received the Ten Commandments from God while camped on a mountain top. When Moses came down from the mountain, Hebrew scribes wrote that Moses had to wear a veil to hide his burned face. It is my contention that while chiseling the text into the stone while using the campfire for light, his face was burnt by the flames emitting the light.

What the Bible and Sunday School teachers plus the ministers did not tell you was the original laws to govern mankind were the two hundred plus laws developed by King Hammurabi of Babylonia. In fact, the phrase Eye for an Eye did not originate with the alleged Moses.

The plagues of Egypt were emulated a number of years past in the African country of Cameroon. A body of water turned red, individuals died sleeping on the floor, insects and boils appeared. There was no curse by an alleged Hebrew Arab prophet but seismic activity. (Individuals forget the planet's surface was formed by the movement of the earth's plates and volcanic eruptions.)

There was not nation of Israel until May 1948. Prior to the establishment of Israel, the Arabs, Hebrews and other ethnic groups of Arabs, allegedly controlled the Kingdom's of Judea and Samaria. However, the scribes and clergy failed to mention that the land of Palestine was part of the Roman Empire.

Moreover, Bible and Sunday School teachers plus ministers teach that Jesus Christ was a Jew. However, to be politically correct, Jesus was a Palestinian. In the real world, a religious affiliation can not be a nationality or race.

And, the automatic assumption that a child born of a woman whose religion is Judaism, Christianity or Islam will be of the same religion as their mother frustrates me. The individual may choose not to believe in a fabricated religious entity.

During my years in the military and employment following retirement in the Kingdom of Saudi Arab and travels to Muslim and former Muslim dominated countries, one learned that religious devotion, in most cases, depends on the religious police or the squadron's religious leader to assure the citizens attend prayer call.

In the United States, I've found that most of the people in my area that claims to be Jews or Christians are probably the most dishonest in the community. In fact, when I was a young man, we used to comment that most citizens went to church to gossip, show of their wealth and, on Easter, wear their new Easter Clothes.

I had one construction contractor when I purchased my home in 2001 that failed to pay a masonry bill and the manufacturer wrote that they may place a lien on my property because the contractor did not pay for the cement blocks. Oh, but the individual told me he went to church at least three times per week and his father was a minister.

And, Kentucky's 5th U.S. Congressional District is one of the worst areas in the nation for welfare fraud, family abuse, and the consumption of illicit drugs. Also, one observes signs that say support our troops or God Bless our Soldiers, yet they sit like sheep and allow our Zionist Congress to send our military off to war to support US Corporations and the state of Israel.

In Kentucky, loyalty to Israel comes before the United States of America. We must send Americans to Congress to end the depression and our country's constant state of aggression.

In recent years, reports are being filed that the European Jew is becoming dissatisfied with the government of Israel and the lack of truth in their promised land. In this light, recently, Even the Central Intelligence Agency published a report stating in the near future Israeli's will be returning to the United States or their country of birth or family ancestry.

June 9, 2011, while scanning the news inputs at OpEdNews, I came across a news item titled, by Mr. Franklin Lamb. In the text, he paraphrased a Jewish Journalist Gideon Levy –"If our Dreamt of an Israeli passport to escape from Europe, there are many among who are now dreaming of a second passport to escape to Europe."

The article continues to give more creditability to the CIA report. For example, a 2008 survey found that 59% of Israelis had approached or intended to approach a foreign embassy to inquire about or apply for citizenship and passport. Today it is estimated that the figure is approaching 70%.

Another study found that more than 100,00 Israelis already hold a German passport, and this figure increases by more than 7,000 every year. German officials report more than 70,000 passports have been granted since 2000.

Now for the Jews contemplating coming to the United States. The document reads there are more than 500,000 Israelis hold US passports, with a quarter of a million pending applications which the US will expeditiously issue. Israeli Arabs need not apply.

The following is a direct quote from the document regarding a second passport as an insurance passport "for the rainy days visible on the horizon." Two of the common denominators are unease and anxiety, both personal and national as one researcher from Eretz Acheret explained. (Eretz Acheret is a non-profit company that published a bi-monthly Hebrew magazine.)

Other factors include:

"*   The fact two or three generations in Israel have not not proven enough to implant roots where few if any existed before. For this reason Israel has produced a significant percentage of "re-immigration" – a return of immigrants or their descendents to their country of origin which Zionist propaganda to the country notwithstanding, is not Palestine."

"*   Fear that religious fanatics from among the more than 600,00 settlers in the West Bank will create civil war and essentially annex pre-1967 Israel and turn more towarad an ultra-fascist state."

"*   Centripetal pressures within Israeli society, especially among Russian immigrants who overwhelmingly reject Zionism. Since the fall of the Berlin Wall in 1969, some one million Jews have come to Israel from the former Soviet Union, enlarging the country's population by 25% and forming the largest concentration in the world of Russian Jews. But today, Russian Jews comprise the largest group emigrating from Israel and they have been returning in droves for reasons ranging from opposition to Zionism, discrimination, and broken promises regarding employment and "the good life" in Israel."

"*   Approximately 200,000 or 22% of Russians coming to Israel since 1990 have so far returned to their country. According to Rabbi Berel Larzar, who has been Russia's chief Rabbi since 2000, "It's absolutely extraordinary how many people are returning. When Jews left, there was no community, no Jewish life. People felt that being Jewish was an historical mistake that happened to their family. Now, they know they can live in Russia as part of a community and they don't need Israel.""

"*   No faith in or respect for Israeli leaders, most of whom are considered corrupt."

"*   Feelings of anxiety and guilt that Zionism has hijacked Judaism and that traditional Jewish values are being corrupted."

"*   The increasing difficulty of providing coherent answers to one's children, ass they become more educated and aware of their family history, and indeed honesty to oneself, on the question of why families from Europe and elsewhere are living on land and in homes stolen from others who obviously are local and did not come from some other place around the world."

"*   The recent growing appreciation, for many Israelis, significantly abetted by the Internet and the continuing Palestinian resistance, of the compelling and challenging Palestinians' narrative that totally undermines the Zionist clarion of the last century of "A land without a People for a People without a Land.""

"*   Fear-mongering of the political leaders designed to keep citizens supporting the government's policies ranging from the Iranian bombs, the countless "Terrorists" seemingly everywhere and planning another Holocaust, or various existential threats that keep families on edge and concluding that they don't want to raise their children under such conditions."

The article continued with what I have been saying since the turmoil in Egypt in that freedom of the people in places like Egypt will result in greater anger against the state of Israel. Already countries of the European Union are questioning the United States intention of vetoing Palestinian statehood in September 2011.

On May 24, 2011, Israeli Prime Minister Netanyahu delivered and arrogant, racist and warmongering speech before both Houses of Congress. (Allegedly, he received multi numbers of standing ovations.) His (Netanyahu) last statements were "Providence (GOD) entrusted the United States to be the guardian of liberty — Thank you for ensuring that the flame of freedom burns bright throughout the world ... May God forever bless the United States of America."

The following are the NOES, Netanyahu addressed regarding the Israeli-Palestinian conflict:

*   "No return to 1967 borders. "The order will be different than the one that existed on June 4, 1967."
On June 5, 1967, Israel launched a surprise attack on Egypt, Syria, and Jordan. Israel occupied the remaining 22 percent of Palestine - the West Bank, Gaza, and East Jerusalem - as well as

Egypt's Sinai Peninsula and Syria's Golan Heights. Netanyahu asserted the right of Israel to keep and expand its illegal settlements on stolen Palestinian land in the West Bank, and much of the Jordan Valley. "It is vital that Israel maintain a long-term military presence along the Jordan River."

* "No right of return for Palestinian refugees. By means of terror, 750,000 Palestinians were driven out to make way for the Israeli state in 1948, their homes, lands and other property confiscated. Today they and their descendents number more than six million, many of whom are still consigned to refugee camps. "This means that the Palestinian refugees problem will be resolved outside the borders of Israel," stated Netanyahu."

* "No to the return of any part of Jerusalem. East Jerusalem was illegally annexed to Israel after the 1967 war and then expanded to take in much additional West Bank land. All Palestinian parties call for Jerusalem to be the capital of a Palestinian state. "Jerusalem must never again be divided. Jerusalem must remain the capital of Israel."

* "No to a Palestinian state that can defend itself. "So it is therefore absolutely vital for Israel's security that a Palestinian state be fully demilitarized." Thanks to the hundreds of billions of dollars of U.S. aid, Israel is ranked as the 4th or 5th military power in the world."

* "No negotiations at all with the Palestinians unless the recently signed Palestinian National Reconciliation Agreement is broken. "So I say to President Abbas, Tear up your pact with Hamas. Sit down and negotiate!""

From the five noes from Prime Minister Netanyahu's speech to Congress we learned US aid to Israel made Israel the 4th or 5th largest military in the world. Also, not identified, Israel possess more than 100 nuclear bombs. (The French government built the nuclear reactors for Israel in the 1950s. Israel threatens Israel with nuclear destruction from the 1960s forward.)

My interests were aroused by the support we provide Israel, so I went to an Internet Web Site and asked the question: How much money did the United States give Israel since 1948? (The web site answered with "How much money did America give Israel since 1948? Partial answers below:

US Aid: The Facts

- The close relationship between the two states is reflected in the volume of aid Israel receives from the US. Since World War II Israel has been the largest overall recipient of US aid: From 1949 - 2006 Israel received more than 156 billion in direct US aid.

- Until 2003, Israel received approximately one-third of the annual US foreign aid budget. In 2005, the US gave Israel more than 2.6 billion in aid, a budget exceeded only by US aid to Iraq. By comparison, Jordan received $683.6 million, Rwanda received $ 77 million, and the Occupied Palestinian Territories received $348.2 million.

- In the past, a majority of the direct US aid to Israel was via US Economic Support Funds (ISF). The US publicly states the ESF are given in order to support stability in areas strategic to the US. However, the recipient government completely controls how it spends these funds.

- The US also lends money to Israel, but the loans are frequently waived before any repayments are made. The Washington Report on Middle East Affairs has estimated that from 1974-2003 Israel benefited from more than $45 billion in waived loans from the US.

- Direct US aid to Israel has significantly diminished since 1996 in order to reduce Israeli financial dependence on the US. Speaking to the US Congress in July 1996, Former Israeli Prime Minister Binyamin Netanyahu declared, "We will begin the long-term process of gradually reducing the level of your generous economic assistance to Israel."

POLITICAL SUPPORT

- The US has a history of giving Israel direct political support. In 1972, the US prevented the adoption of UN resolution S/10784 paragraph 74, which condemned Israeli attacks against southern Lebanon and Syria. In order to do this, the US used its veto power in the Security Council for only the second time.

- Since 1972, the US has used the veto power to prevent the adoption of 42 UN resolutions that condemned or severely criticized actions by the State of Israel. In 2006, for example, the US prevented the adoption of UN resolution S/878 which demanded a mutual ceasefire in the Gaza Strip.

-        In 2002, former US Ambassador to the United Nations, John Negroponte, stated that it was the US policy to denounce all UN resolutions that criticized Israel without also condemning "terrorist groups." This statement is now known as the Negroponte-doctrine.

Military Aid

-        Whilst US economic aid to Israel has diminished in the last ten years, the level of US military support to Israel has substantially increased.

-        This includes financial military aid.

-        Israel's military superiority is largely dependent on various forms of direct US support, including financial military aid and donations, weapons deliveries and technological support.

As a concerned American I have been monitoring our aid, in whatever the form, for a long time. In a paragraph above, the word donation was mentioned. My countrymen, Zionist (Jewish zealots and Old Testament Christians) provide billions of dollars in direct monetary contributions and, equally important, through their efforts elected individuals to Congress and the Executive Office that have no morals and without honor. The individuals sell you and I out for money, ancestral heritage and religion.

Moreover, the news media report quite often, but national news want print the information, that Congress provided Israel with $200 plus million for research on missile systems for Israel.

An Israeli company now manufacturers and sells the Drones used in Afghanistan instead of an American manufacturer.

The Israelis have sold military technology to foreign nations, especially China.

The Department of Defense dispatches U.S. missile personnel at the drop of a hat to man missile site in Israel. In truth, our military personnel and Americans whose religion is Judaism augment the Israeli military in some fashion in every conflict since the establishment of the State of Israel.

My fellow Americans it is past time for the Congress of the United States and whichever Presidential Administration in power at the time to announce a national policy of:

ENFORCING THE SEPARATION OF CHURCH AND STATE

-   Individuals of any religion, especially Judaism, can no longer identify themselves by their religious affiliation. We are Americans, not hyphenated Americans or religious zealots.

-   Religious organizations, regardless of affiliation, and the every day American citizen can no longer support any foreign nation or their population through any type of donation/support etc. Said violation will result in the party and/or parties charged with subversion and/or sedition.

-   All Foreign Aid given to Israel or Egypt will be terminated forthwith.

-   Congress will pass legislation and the President will

sign, stating that no American may hold a dual citizenship nor shall they be able to serve in the military of a foreign nation.

- The Congress will submit legislation, which the President will sign, declaring the United States of America is a Constitutional Democracy and that our nation is religion neutral.

REMINDER OF THE COST FREEDOM FOR OUR REPUBLIC - THE UNITED STATES OF AMERICA

In my home county in Kentucky, population approximately 36,000, the majority of present day residents have never suffered the trials and tribulations of a combat zone. However, there are those that remember the rationing and ration stamps from World War II. But, in truth, Laurel County didn't suffer, except for gas rations and products not grown on the family farms.

The country was rural, not manufacturing, the farmers raised tobacco and hemp for out of state distribution. Gardens and farm animals provided a good life for southern and southeastern Kentuckians. The only factory type employment during my childhood, that I remember, was Kerns Bread, a fertilizer plant and a church furniture factory.

Of course, during World War II, a large number of residents of Laurel County were drafted. Korea we provided our share. Vietnam has short of names on a hurtful marker, in front of the court house, of those draftees and volunteers that died in Vietnam. The illegal wars of Korea and Vietnam, Laurel County sends probably more than their share to enlist in the military. Some enlist (ed) for pride and love of country, others enlist for a chance to better themselves through education, be employed, or just get away from, in some areas, a racist and negative environment.

Laurel County is one of those Kentucky Counties where religion was passed down from one generation. Each succeeding generation took what was passed down as to be the truth. Never suspecting, their Bible, Torah, or Koran were written by men with their own self-interest. Their response to their environment, good or bad, it's the will of God.

These same people that depend on God for their life, liberty and pursuit of happiness are the ones that attempt forcefully or otherwise to demand Americans identify the United States as a Christian Nation. Our country has never been a Christian Country.

Let us go back to the first non-indigenous persons that set foot on North America. Some say Norsemen visited first, Then of course came the many adventurers from Spain. The Queen Isabella of Spain paid for Columbus' voyage. (Of course there were others, for we do not know.)

But, the really true adventurers were the trappers, hunters, and those seeking wealth and power. Kentucky, for example, was a greedy and prosperous person's dream come true. Animal furs, fish, salt, women to marry and land to homestead were for the taking. Yes, there were other ethnic groups sent in by the East India Trading Company, Dutch Trading, etc. Daniel Boone was paid by a trader from Pennsylvania to settle in the Kentucky Wilderness. Greed and self satisfaction settled Kentucky and the rest of the western United States.

After western's became a part of the landscape, more greedy individuals came but in their minds, they brought the religion for a fabricated God that was already responsible for the murder of the American native. Oh, one must not forget. The new comer's religious books approved of people of color being bought and sold as slaves.

By the 1640, the religionist had turned their religious zealotry against their own community. Finally, government cut off the money to the religious leaders and some civility came to the settlers. No longer put in stocks or burnt at the stake.

After life became better than it was in Europe for many, a group of upper middle class and wealthy colonist, who also were highly educated both academic and of the international community. These individuals, although not in the majority, introduced the colonist to the Declaration of Independence. (Photo, public domain, provided for review.)

The declaration charged the King of British Empire with charges against, in today words, humanity and declared we will be free of the monarchy. War came and the colonist won with massive support from the French government.

The colonist that fought to rid the colonies of the British were rewarded, once we had an established government, not by money but tracks of land. To this date, there are Kentuckians whose ancestors were granted land for their support of the revolution.

A number of years past, I went to Philadelphia, PA, the home of Independence Hall to see for myself the environment our founders chose to move our nation forward.

As most Americans, I supposed, I went into Independence Hall with a tour guide. The view of the building and the interior brought chill bumps. However, being my usual self, I saw a picture of a large bird hanging. I asked the tour guide what kind of bird it was. She said it was a Bald Eagle. I was set back, the bird sure didn't look our national bird. In fact, I told her the picture looked more like a Vulture than a Bald Eagle.

Regarding the Bald Eagle, we learned that Benjamin Franklin, one of our most vocal founders, disliked the Bald Eagle. His choice, to his daughter in a letter, was for the Turkey.

Of note, prior to writing this chapter, I scanned the internet and printed pictures, public domain, of the famous structures and of an Eagle and Turkey for those that have not been to Philadelphia.

From Philadelphia, I fast forward to another site in Pennsylvania with a terrible, violent, and heartbreaking history - Gettysburg, PA.

At this location, was battle fought between two American Armies. One from the North, Union, and the second from the South, the Confederacy. Worse yet, in some battles on opposite sides, family members fought each other. Americans were fighting each other in a Civil War. (Photos, public domain, are provided for review.)

There are those Americans that say the Civil War was because of slavery. I do not believe that the owning of slaves was without questions among individuals from both the North and South. From the families, still living in Kentucky that I have personal knowledge from research I conducted, I do not believe the owners were malice in way when dealing with slaves, whether indentured slaves or the purchased slave at an auction.

The reason I made the statement about malice is that many farmers and land owners were hand-me down religious Christian. The clergy and religious associations said the religious books stated it was ok to own slaves. (Our next civil war in the United States will be over which religion's God is the most powerful and correct.) The clergy went as far as to identify Christ as white with Blue eyes.

From 1865, we advance to December 1, 1941, the Japanese bomb Pearl Harbor, HI. September 1945, the Japanese high command surrenders of the USS Missouri. Millions of lives lost through death or re-location. US Allies prevailed. (Photo, public domain, provided for review.)

The United States is now one of the leading voices at the United Nation. Harry S. Truman is President. North Korea attacks South Korea. Truman sends in US forces to defeat the North Koreans. General MacArthur wants to drive into Communist China, the President say no. President Truman fires MacArthur. President Dwight David Eisenhower replaces Truman and a truce is made with the North Koreans and Chinese. Still no official ending of the Korean War.

Korean War Memorial built in Washington, DC. United Nations (UN) War. (Photo, public domain, provided for review.)

French defeated in South Vietnam. United States enters the war from a lie told by President Lyndon B. Johnson. Southeast Asia Treaty Organization (SEATO) War. (Photo, public domain, provided for review.)

From the Korean War forward, our country has dispatched forces to: Iran, Lebanon, Somalia, Panama, Grenada, Falkland Islands, Saudi Arabia, Kuwait, Iraq, Kuwait, Afghanistan, Vietnam, Cambodia, Laos, Thailand and I'm sure there are other I've missed.

No Declaration of War was declared by the Congress of the United States. Congress abdicated their Constitutional requirement to declare war at the end of World War II. I suppose the reason why is that certain members of Congress were probably responsible for many of the military deployments. We know, beyond a shadow of a doubt, that the 1998 Iraq Resolution Act was responsible for both the invasion of Afghanistan and Iraq.

I can not address the rest of the nation but for Kentucky's 5th Congressional District, I am somewhat of an expert. To this end, my fellow Kentuckians are as much to blame for the deaths of the American military and citizens, both military and civilian, of the countries our military invaded without just cause.

June 2011, according to the news paper, Kentucky's National Guard was deployed, largest since World War II, to Iraq. The Constitution states the Milita (National Guard) may be activated for two reasons: (1) to put down an insurrection. (2) Repeal an opposing armed force attacking the United States. Neither of the two occurred.

Yes, Congress, I believe in 1947, worked out illegal agreements with the states to utilize the National Guard as part of the US active duty forces. The citizen/soldier became a mercenary to the Oil Companies and Zionist. (No Constitutional Amendment.)

I am an atheist but should there be a God and Hell, those that do not raise up their voices against the actions of the United States Congress, should burn in Hell.

SEPTEMBER 11, 2001, THE ULTIMATE ACT OF TREASON

POLITICIANS EXEMPT FROM PROSECUTION

I don't understand how the United States Justice Department can prosecute Americans, for crimes such as possession of marijuana, while individuals like former President George W. Bush and Vice President Richard Cheney's actions and lack of action resulted in the deaths of an unknown number of individuals on September 11, 2001. Only time will tell, the number of citizens that will die from exposure to toxic air and debris encountered during and following the aerial attacks.

June 14, 2011, while scanning the Internet for news releases, I came across the best reporting on the 9/11 incident ever. The name of the publication was An On-Line Journal. The report was in four parts: 9-11 and the IMPOSSIBLE - the Pentagon, 9-11 and the IMPOSSIBLE - Flight 93, 9-11 and the impossible - the WTC and 9-11 and the IMPOSSIBLE - The Bizarre Politics of 9-11.

The publication broke down each of the three incidents and the politics involved. There are photos and illustrations that dispute our governments report of events. The text of the parts are blunt and do not cower should there be a agency that punishes individuals for telling the truth.

The same afternoon, I read another news release title "Pro-Israeli Turning U.S. into Islamophobic Police State." Part of the text addressed the introduction of the Homeland Security Act and the Patriot Act. From the On Line Journal, we learned the Homeland Security Act and the Patriot Act were written in the Clinton Administration.

In the same article, Senator Chuck's Schumer interview with a Jewish radio talk show host in New York confirmed my belief that Schumer is a traitor to the United States by his words, For example, Senator Schumer said "he believed that HaShem, an Orthodox Jewish term for "GOD" gave him the name "Schumer" — which means "Guardian" so he could fulfill his "very Important" role in the US Senate as a "Guardian of Israel." Presumably, Schumer's God-given role also includes turning the country he is actually paid to represent — the United States — into an Islamophobic police state."

Moreover, there is a Patriot II waiting in the wings written by Congressman Hastert, Attorney General Ashcroft, and Richard Cheney. I supposed we should be thankful Patriot Act II was implemented - just an extension of the first Patriot Act.

Another interesting fact, we learned reading new releases on June 14, 2011 were the alleged words of former US Ambassador to Iraq, Ms. April Glaspie. We learned "Taking April Glaspie at her 1991 words, Saddam was expected to only take Kuwait's Northern Oil Fields, not the whole country. Thus, her admonishment that the US had no position on inter-Arab affairs is left in the light of the US enables Saddam – until he got greedy."

And, my fellow Americans, what I've written take from the On Line Journal is just a drop in the bucket. As Americans you should read the entire series of articles and any other identified by the Journal. Our country was sold out by so called Americans in Congress and the White House.

Oh, there is one part of the Journal that I don't agree regarding remote control of an airliner. For example, I read were the Boeing 757 and 767 were designed; whereas, control of the aircraft could be taken over. With regards to taxing an aircraft by remote control, the writer didn't feel that act was possible. This where I disagree. The reason I disagree is that US Air Force pilots taxi, take-off, orbit, land, and taxi the drones used in Afghanistan from a Continent away.

Moreover, on a personal experience level of 20 years in the Air Operations Military Career Field, of which 6 were in the Kingdom of Saudi Arabia training Saudi Warrant Officers in Air Operations. As an operations person, you work with aircrews in their flight training, proficiency flights, and administer their flight records. Each pilot must have an established number of events flown under the eye of a Flight Examiner. Therefore based on my experience, along with the same words from both US Air Force and civilian pilots, no Boeing 757 could have flown the route of flight identified by Congressional report. Impossible.

On a true personal note, during my career, I was afforded the opportunity to sit in the left seat of two USAF aircraft - the L-20 (Beaver) and the T-39 (Saber) Jet. For example, to reduce your altitude in the L-20 you used more yoke pressure than you did in the T-39. In the Saber Jet, you only tapped the yoke to descend. Greater pressure would result in a greater loss of altitude.

And, with respect, regarding the Saudis that attended flight school in the US in a single engine, top wing small training aircraft, there was no way they could go aboard a 757 and accomplish the charge of flying into the Pentagon.

Americans please contact your members of Congress

and demand respectfully that former President Bush and Vice President Cheney be brought up on the charge of TREASON.

With regards to Senator Schumer and the other members of Congress that possess dual citizenship and/or claim their loyalty to Israel, they should be prosecuted.

UNITED STATES NATIONALISTS WORKER'S PARTY

The time has long past for the formation of a political party where the members are Americans. Members only goal is to further the American dream for all our countrymen. No more corporate wars, no more religious crusades, no more actual poverty, and no defaults and/or credit down grades of the United States dollar.

The new political party will be the United States Nationalists Worker's Party (USNWP). American workers manufacturing for Americans consumption and export to nations that pay for the products. No more gifts, until our economy is once again the envy of the international community.

There was a time when our country had three financially based classes of Americans.

The Middle Class were the auto workers, factory workers, small town merchants, returning military veterans that earned a college degree, those individuals seeking the American dream and, of course, the clergy. Their vision was to make their children's lives better than theirs.

The Upper Class Americans, the rich, were those that inherited money from the earlier years of the United States when our country's advancement were led by money changers, cotton barons, railroad tycoons, shipping magnets, industrialist such as Henry Ford, and, of course, John D. Rockefeller's oil.

A new wealth came from the inventions by German scientist recovered by US agencies following World War II. Transfer of dual use products made by and for the US military to the domestic consumer. Moreover, some say, a number of scientific advancements were made from the reverse engineering of alien space craft recovered by the US Government in New Mexico.

Within decades of World War II, a new industry emerged in Silicon Valley, California. This industry introduced to world: Micro-Soft, Apple, Intel, etc. In this light, the great International Business Machine Corporation (IBM) had to step aside.

Sadly, in my opinion, a recent news release reported that 400 individuals in the United States of America possessed more wealth than the other 320 million plus residents of the United States.

For the poor growing up in southern and southeastern Kentucky, the disparity between Kentucky's industrial north and our region was visibly apparent in all areas of life. Even our education system was different from the rest of the state. Our economy was based on agriculture while the other areas of the state had industry, horse farms and federal government manufacturing and/or US Military Installations.

Our home life didn't compare with the city dwellers. Many of us at different periods did not have running water in the home. The bathroom was an outhouse near the home. Home television was a rarity. Only the upper class poor or the middle class owned televisions. Some Kentuckians walked to school while others rode a bus for an hour or more. Going to the movies and listening to Elvis depended on how deeply parents placed the words of the clergy ahead of their children.

However, the one act imposed by the poor was that family members got out of bed and went to work at whatever job was available. Family men and young single men would work all day in a tobacco field or gather hay for $5.00 per day and a plentiful lunch.

Other poor not within walking distance to seasonal labor scratched out their living from the hillsides, hollers, and, if lucky, flat land. They raised a garden and chickens. If lucky, there may be a pig or cow to provide additional meat.

Family members would pick blackberries for pies and other sweets. (One could find blackberries growing throughout the mountains and hollers.) For other meats than raised on the farms, Kentuckians remained great hunters and fishermen. great hunters and fisherman.

Yes, some accepted government cheese, beans and powered milk that continued after the war years. However, although they chose to be independent, they remained Americans.

For many, like myself, our mother or father signed for us to enter the Armed Forces of the United States as soon as we turned 17 years old. We departed, as others did for the industrial north, the region to further our education, on our own, and earn a retirement living. After retirement, still a mountain person, we returned to our region of birth.

In 1960s, Lyndon B. Johnson and Robert Kennedy, both candidates for the Office of US Chief Executive, came to eastern Kentucky. From these visits came Washington's Poverty Act - a social welfare system.

With a doubt, many Kentuckians knew they were poor but still attempted to be honest and work when they could. With Washington's gimmick to buy votes, the federal, state, and county governments rated families based on their financial status. For example, for a family to receive the benefits of the welfare system, a household was rated by the number of individuals in their household versus their financial income. After your financial and household status were ascertained, governments determined you should have said number of dollars and benefits to remain above an artificially imposed poverty line.

President Lyndon B. Johnson, Great Society, and his

administrators did not learn from Roman History. For example, when the Roman Government began supplying Rome's population with food, the poor in the country, moved into the cities and/or became dependant on their government to provide subsistence. Millions throughout the United States, especially in Kentucky, are emulating Rome's history of Socialism.

In Kentucky's 5th US Congressional District (counties of southern and eastern Kentucky) too many have become proficient in abusing our government's attempt at socialism. For example, the fraudulent users receive a government monetary check monthly, food stamps, Section 8 Housing Assistance, climate control funds, and gratis health care via a government Medicaid or Medicare Card.

There are school age children that receive back packs filled with food items for when school is not in session. Churches and other charity groups hand out clothing, schools supplies and other items at designated periods during the year.

Please step back. The truth is that most Americans, not born wealthy and continued their wealth, have at one time or another in their life asked for subsistence from another entity. The entity may not have been government funded but a family or friend. However, their situation did not continue for generations.

And, for the record, the US Constitution does not guarantee

any gratis items for Life, Liberty and the Pursuit of Happiness. Each state with their state's rights may assist their citizens. However, it is not the responsibility of other states in the Union to subsidize another state's failure to administer their population. For example, the last reading, revealed for every $1.00 Kentuckians send to the federal government, we receive $1.51 back from the treasury.

The political candidates and the Congress of the United States dreamed up more ways to spend the taxpayers money without representation. One of the new ways was to devise a student loan program and educational grants for college students. However, from first hand observation, the loan and grant programs are more avenues to defraud the American taxpayers.

Yes, the American people have the willingness to support the nation's college age students and those Americans, for whatever the reason, seek out a college education later in life. However, what good is a Bachelor of Science or Masters Degree when there are not jobs available and/or the student will not seek employment out of state or outside the United States. For some it is either employment within their county, or welfare.

For example of educational abuse, the wife, of an unemployed eastern Kentuckian, in her late 30s or early 40s, has mastered the art of fraud and welfare abuse. Her and her family's primary income is the money received from educational grants and under the table employment.

The family receives food stamps and has a medical card.

The year of 2011, the woman, her daughters, and three friends went on a cruise to the Bahamas, attended a race in the Carolinas, gave birth to child for the state or federal government to raise. The three friends are subsistence abusers as well.

Babies are now the avenue to not become employed and DRAW. (DRAW - receive unearned monetary compensation from a government agency.) In this light, it appears the religious communities throughout the Red State prefer the biblical directive "it is better to place your seed in the belly of a whore than place it on the ground" than allow the distribution of condoms and sex education in our school systems.

A Case and Point regarding something from nothing recently made the news in Kentucky and probably the nation. The Case two young ladies in their twenties are suing the federal government to obtain Social Security Cards.

One of the ladies was born in Kentucky at home. The second was, allegedly, born in an automobile in Alabama. They now reside in Lily, Kentucky.

Photographs of the ladies sitting at the entrance to a residence were well dressed and appeared knowledgeable of proper posture.

The Point is that from birth a great number in our country learn they can become obese, lazy, under educated, a drug addict, an alcoholic, etc.; whereas, the government will provide their subsistence.

Note: a year or so past, a transplanted New York City lady was working as a waitress at London's Airport Café. Part time she was assisting at Sue Bennett College tutoring individuals attempt to pass their GED Test. One student made the statement he wanted to DRAW. The lady made the effort to purchase art supplies for the student. He told no he didn't want to be an artist, he wanted to receive a gratis check from the government. DRAW.

Returning to college grants and student loans. Yes, without a doubt, the American people have the willingness to support the nation's college age students and those Americans, for whatever the reason, seek out a college education later in life. However, what good is a Bachelor of Science or Masters Degree when there are no jobs available and the student will not seek employment out of state or outside the United States?

And, on par with the lack of employment, in the Red States, a student's mind is cluttered with the untruths presented by those who claim to believe in a Supreme Being or the God of Abraham. What is worse, these fabricators place the loyalty to their religious entity ahead of the founding documents of this great nation: the

Declaration of Independence and the U.S. Constitution.

The Declaration of Independence and the U.S. Constitution are in the top four documents, in my opinion, ever written by man. The top two are the Code of Hammurabi and the Magna Charter. These documents identified that no man is superior to another and that each of us have equal rights in a civilized society.

However, over time, even the most honorable endeavor becomes corrupted. In fact, our founders, especially Thomas Jefferson knew what greed and power would do to a person without honor and integrity. To this end, paraphrasing President Jefferson "there will times in our country's history that the people will have to rise up and replace the government with a new government."

The time to replace the government with a new government came early in my lifetime with the election of Harry S. Truman as President of the United States of American. No, I do not remember first hand what Truman did as I was only one year and five months old when Truman assumed the Presidency at the death of President Franklin D. Roosevelt. However, from research I learned that in May 1948, he was the first American President, in my opinion, to commit TREASON against the people of the United States of America.

Right away there are those crying foul. To clarify for those doubters, the following is a quote of Article 3, Section 3

Treason from the US Constitution: "Treason against the United States, shall consist only in levying War against them, or in adhering to their enemies, giving them Aid and Comfort. No Person shall be convicted of Treason unless on the Testimony of two Witness to the same overt Act, or on Confession in open Court."

My logic for the charge of TREASON:

1. The most important fact is that the United States of America was in May 1948 and continues to this date, August 16, 2011, a Constitutional Republic. We are not now nor has this nation ever been a Christian, Jewish, Muslim, Buddhist or any other religion's nation. We are secular.

2. President Harry S. Truman should have known, as our founders did, that religion, especially Jewish stories from the Bible and Torah, were responsible for the deaths and dislocation of millions and the occupation of foreign lands. For example, the, alleged, Prophet Moses ordered his family members and followers to go into Canaan (Palestine) and kill everyone, except for virgins, and occupy their land. The Acts were, allegedly, at the orders of the God of Abraham. Christian murders came later in the form of European Crusaders to kill, maim the people Palestine and occupy their land.

3. President Truman should have known from early American history, in New Amsterdam, individuals of

Judaism did not consider themselves a citizen of their host country but as the "Wandering Jew Plant," a parasite.

4. As a soldier in World War I in Europe fighting the German Army and the aftermath of the Treaty of Versailles, Truman should have known our entry into World War I was forced upon our nation by Zionists Bankers and a Jewish blackmailer.

5. Truman should have known the Zionist who paid for his election campaign and their religious voting bloc put him into the White House wanted something for their actions.

6. Truman's mother surely influenced his decision to recognize Israel due to her schooling at a Baptist College. Hand me down religious beliefs.

7. Truman should not have allowed his personal friendship with his life long friend and business partner, Eddie Jacobson, to influence his decision to recognize the armed Jewish setters occupying the land of Palestine as the state of Israel.

8. Following Truman's recognition of Israel, his administration provided billions to the illegal occupiers of Palestine. The hell with our economy that just recovered from a Great Depression.

9. Regarding witness, there were many more than two that urged President Truman not to recognize Israel. (Secretary

of State George Marshall, the Chiefs of Military Staff, career State Department Officials, etc. advised against his actions.) His administration knew, in my opinion, he was committing TREASON.

Yes! My definition may be broad but from May 15, 1948 forward our nation continues to loose its treasure based on a fabricated GOD and uninformed citizens.

And, using my definition, every President of the United States of America, in my lifetime, have violated their Oath of Office to the American people. Equally guilty are the member of Congress with their dual loyalty and adherence to their religious teachings instead of the US Constitution.

In September 2011, the Palestinian Authority will, allegedly, seek recognition of statehood at the United Nations. From news releases and web site traffic, our government is threatening, blackmailing, and paying off nations, in some form, for their vote to deny Palestine their Mother Nature Right to be a nation within he community of nations.

One should remember Palestine has been on the world map for centuries. Israel became an illegal state on May 15, 1948. What you read in the Bible or any other book regarding the nation of Israel is a lie.

So, to return our country to the dictates of the Declaration of Independence and US Constitution, the only way to do so, in my opinion, is to initiate a new political party that will return to our country's government to the founding father's visions - THE UNITED STATES NATIONALIST WORKERS PARTY.

COMMENTS

Please bear with me regarding the text. I'm sure there are a large number of redundancy which I apologize. I am not a writer just a retired Air Force Air Operations Superintendent that wants his country back. Please forgive.

In one of the chapters, I wrote that I was a Deist but that title was months past. I am an Atheist. There are too many facts being uncovered that identifies the God of Abraham as a fraud and the religious writings are fabrications to make the particular ethnic groups appear superior to the other Arabs in Palestine.

The illustration with the text Religious Subversion was paid for by me. Previous inclusion was in a second book "Enough Is Enough."

The founders of this great nation were educated academically and from first hand experiences in the capitals of Europe. Their words in the Declaration of Independence and the US Constitution are as applicable today as they were in colonial days.

EQUALITY, LIFE, LIBERTY, AND THE PURSUIT OF HAPPINESS

"Whenever any form of government becomes destructive to these ends, it is the right of the people to alter or to abolish it, and to institute new government." Thomas Jefferson

"I am mortified to be told that, in the United States of America, the sale of a book can become a subject of inquiry, and of criminal inquiry too." Thomas Jefferson

RELIGION

"All national institutes of churches, whether Jewish, Christian, or Turkish, appear to me no other than human inventions set up to terrify and enslave mankind, and monopolize power and profit." Thomas Paine.

Every American has the right to or not worship any entity as their GOD or Supreme Being. However, when that entity becomes superior in loyalty to the United States of America, then the people must rise up and end the subversion. Billy Ray Wilson.